Cultivating Communities Series

Book Three

The Form of the Word

Making Sense of Scripture in the Body of Christ

by Stephen E. Fowl

ENGLEWOODPRESS.COM

Copyright © 2025 by Stephen E. Fowl
Originally published in an alternate form as a digital resource by The Ekklesia Project.

Published by Englewood Press
57 N. Rural Street
Indianapolis, IN 46201

www.englewoodpress.com

All rights reserved.

No portion of this book may be reproduced in any form without written permission from the publisher or author, except as permitted by U.S. copyright law.

ISBN 978-1-934406-24-3 (print)
ISBN 978-1-934406-25-0 (digital)

Library of Congress Control Number: 2025939664

Unless otherwise noted, scripture quotations contained herein are from *The New Revised Standard Version Updated Edition,* Copyright © 2021, by the Division of Christian Education of the National Council of Churches in the United States of America.

Cover design: Eliza Whyman

Praise for *The Form of the Word: Making Sense of Scripture in the Body of Christ*

"Too often we read a verse, a passage, or even an entire book of Scripture in isolation. Steve Fowl gives all Christians an important framework for understanding the Bible as a whole. Especially designed for congregations, this perceptive and readable volume from an eminent scholar with a pastoral heart includes appropriate prayers and discussion questions. Highly recommended!"

-Michael J. Gorman, Ph.D.
Raymond E. Brown Chair in Biblical and Theological Studies
St. Mary's Seminary & University, Baltimore

"Christians and congregations are always being formed—by culture, by habits, by stories. *The Form of the Word* helps ensure we're formed by Scripture. With clarity and pastoral depth, Stephen Fowl invites leaders and communities into the drama of salvation—not as spectators, but as participants shaped by God's story. This is a timely, practical guide for churches hungry to grow in biblical literacy, theological imagination, and Christlike formation."

-Lisa Rodriguez-Watson
National Director, Missio Alliance

Contents

The Cultivating Communities Series	VII
Introduction	3
1. Fitting Scripture's Pieces within a Framework	15
2. The Beginning	25
3. The End is the Beginning	31
4. The Call of Abraham	37
5. A People	47
6. Land and Jubilee	61
7. Holiness	69
8. Idolatry	77
9. Steadfast Love	85
10. Jesus, the Redeemer of Israel	93
11. Death and Resurrection	101
12. The Spirit and Scripture	109
Conclusion	119

The Cultivating Communities Series

Our human bodies bear witness to the truth of our lives: to the many sorts of care we have given them or to joys and traumas that they have survived. Similarly, social bodies also bear witness. They take the shape of their members' desires, convictions, and stories. And our churches are no exception. Ideally, our congregations will take a shape that bears witness to the life, death, resurrection, and teachings of Jesus. But all too often that witness is distorted by other loves and other desires in the midst of church communities that don't look a whole lot like Jesus of Nazareth. Nationalism and greed are two such loves that dilute and distort the Christian witness of churches.

In an age dominated by deep social divides – between the political right and left; between rich and poor; between various racial and ethnic identities, between generations; and between educational backgrounds, to name just a few – how is it even possible that a church might have any shape at all beyond the nearly amorphous form taken by the loose network of her individual members?

Beyond these deep divides and the existential threat they pose to our congregations, I am hopeful churches can still mature into the full stature of a body that bears a striking resemblance to Jesus. This maturing is a slow process that will not only take time but also hard work and intentionality. What shape will our individual bodies take if we neglect to care for their physical and mental well-being? Similarly, our churches must be attentive to tending and cultivating our life together, seeking day-by-day, month-by-month, and year-by-year to more fully embody Jesus together in our particular place. This work of patient cultivation lies at the heart of **congregational formation.**

In many ways the contours of congregational formation parallel those of personal spiritual formation. Both congregational and personal formation are driven by the desire to more fully know and embody Jesus, and both take the shape of intentional practices that serve to form us into Christlikeness. However, congregational formation can be particularly messy because it requires the alignment of the desires of multiple people, not just one person. Efforts to align desires by emotional manipulation, or by more authoritarian tactics, will undoubtedly fail with time because their means are decidedly *not* those of the patient love and compassion of Jesus. In these cases, formation does happen, but the shape that is emerging looks little like Jesus.

Indeed, congregational formation occurs as we learn to be attentive to God's presence in us and among us in the Holy Spirit. We learn through a multitude of practices, especially conversation, to share our convictions, our hopes, and our stories together. And we learn to receive one another with gratitude as a vital means of God's provision for shaping and sustaining our life together. Just as our personal bodies constantly adapt, discern, mature, and move through the world as an intricate network of conversations, so also conversation becomes the way that our churches discern together who our members are, how we will care for our collective body, and how we strive to embody Christ together in ways that our neighbors see and become curious about the way of Jesus.

This new Cultivating Communities Series of books serves to offer churches tools for the long journey of congregational formation. These books are intended as field guides to help orient your congregation through essential conversations on this journey. This series is the fruit of a collaborative effort between Cultivating Communities (an initiative designed to assist churches in the work of congregational formation, based at Englewood Christian Church in Indianapolis), Missio Alliance, and the Ekklesia Project. Cultivating Communities is funded by a grant from the Lilly Endowment's Thriving Congregations Initiative, and a portion of this generous funding has been used to launch this new series of books.

The first book in this series, *The Shape of Our Lives*, was published in October 2024 and is a revised and updated edition of a resource originally produced in 2008 by the Ekklesia Project, which introduces the key elements and dynamics of congregational formation. Written by a team of pastors and theological/biblical scholars, including Phil Kenneson, Deborah Dean Murphy, Jenny Williams, Stephen Fowl, and James Lewis, *The Shape of Our Lives* serves not only as a primer on congregational formation, but also a theological backdrop for the subsequent books in this series.

The Virtue of Dialogue is the second book in the series. It builds upon our conviction that conversation is the central practice of congregational formation and recounts the earliest years of Englewood Christian Church's journey of learning to grow together in conversation. We hope this story will provide imagination for many churches about how they might learn to talk and grow together within their own particular contexts.

Subsequent volumes in the series will address specific key facets of congregational formation, including how to read scripture together, how to think and talk about money in our congregations, and more. Each volume will incorporate discussion questions intended to spark conversation. Although each book can be read and reflected on by individual church leaders, this series is primarily intended to be read, prayed over, and discussed by groups within a congregation, including perhaps in some settings, the congregation as a whole. We hope the very form of these books is consistent with and serves to cultivate vital congregational conversations.

C. Christopher Smith
Series Editor

Series Partners

Cultivating Communities is a growing network of people committed to place-based congregational formation. Our team is committed to walking with congregations who desire to cultivate a deeper life together in Christ, which overflows into tangible love for the communities in which they are embedded. Cultivating Communities is funded by a grant from the Lilly Endowment's Thriving Congregations Initiative.

Learn more at **CultivatingCommunities.com.**

The Ekklesia Project is a community of Christians from across the ecclesial spectrum who have found life-giving friendship through a shared hope in the vision of God's good shalom. In the early 2000s, the Ekklesia Project launched the Congregational Formation Initiative (CFI) to nurture and support congregations committed to making lifelong formation and discipleship central to their life together.

Connect online at **EkklesiaProject.org.**

Missio Alliance is a Managing Partner in the Cultivating Communities initiative. Founded in 2011, Missio Alliance offers in-depth theological and practical direction for many pastors and church leaders attempting to navigate the challenges of ministry in a culturally dynamic, post-Christianizing era.

Learn more at **MissioAlliance.org.**

Author's Note

It has been many years since I first worked on the *The Form of the Word*. Thanks to the kind invitation of Chris Smith, I have the opportunity to revisit this work and revise it. The passage of time has allowed me to return to this text with fresh eyes. I remain as convinced now, as I was then, that as Christians engage scripture as an integral part of their life with God, they benefit from being able to fit their study of Scripture into a larger scriptural framework. I think this is true even if people adopt a framework different from the one I present here.

One of the things I appreciate now in ways I did not when I first wrote *The Form of the Word* is the important role of context in Christians' reading of scripture. I am thinking both of my context and the context of those communities who will use this work. The place from which I write shapes my writing and thinking in ways I only partly recognize. As a result, the words here may not connect or only partially connect with readers in very different contexts. In that light, it is important that those who facilitate the use of this text in congregations feel the freedom to modify and adjust things to suit their particular situation.

I have had the privilege of being able to devote significant portions of my career to researching and writing about scripture, theology, and life of the church. I have always relied heavily on the insights, criticisms, and suggestions of friends. Without them, my work would be impoverished. For this relatively short project I have benefitted from the blessings of a dear former colleague and of my newest colleague. Rebekah Eklund, Professor of Theology at Loyola University Maryland and Rachel Toombs, Assistant Professor of Old Testament at Church Divinity School of the Pacific, generously took time to read and comment on a first revision of this work. Their input has enriched this work significantly, and I am grateful for that. Needless to say, the mistakes, errors, and problems with this work are solely my own.

Introduction

Welcome to this study on the shape of scripture. Whether you have been reading the Bible for a long time or just beginning, thinking about the *shape* of scripture may seem strange. One of the first things to do in this introduction is to explain what people might mean when they talk about the shape of scripture. In addition, we will try to offer some comments about matters that might arise in the course of using this material.

Just looking at the table of contents of your Bible is enough to indicate the great variety of texts within the book's cover. Each of these texts on its own rewards the time and effort invested by attentive, prayerful readers. Even so, the more one engages the individual pieces of scripture the more one is faced with the question, "How do all of the books of the Bible hang together?" Is there some sort of overall framework that can help communities of believers grasp a common story line that unites the individual books of the Bible? When we talk about the shape of scripture, we are talking about just such a framework within which Christians might fit the diverse writings that comprise the Bible. The shape of scripture is a way of talking about how all of the different books of the Bible hang together.

You might well wonder: Is such a framework really necessary? One of the aims of the first chapter is to provide some answers to that question (though it may take a couple of chapters to address it adequately). Here in this introduction, we will explore ways of situating scripture as a whole into an account of what God is doing in the world from creation through to redemption. That is, we will consider scripture's relationship to our salvation and to God's desires for the world. Gaining some clarity around these considerations may also help to answer this question of why a framework for reading scripture might be beneficial.

It is a fundamental precept of Christianity that God has given us scripture as part of God's plan to bring us to salvation. Let us try to unpack what such a claim might mean. First, we need to think a bit about what Christians mean by "salvation." This may be a thorny topic for any congregation. In his book *The Virtue of Dialogue,* C. Christopher Smith told the story of how conversation became an essential practice at Englewood Christian Church, but not without sometimes tumultuous conversations around these core tenets of the Christian faith. Smith writes, "One of the most volatile streams of our conversation was our discussion of the nature of salvation. This is not surprising, because salvation is a concept that lies close to the heart of evangelical Christianity."

There are a variety of ways in which Christians, even those sitting next to you, might talk about salvation. Moreover, various Christian groups have their own distinctive terms and phrases when it comes to speaking about salvation. What is said here should not contradict those terms and phrases. At the same time, the things mentioned here are central components of all accounts of salvation worthy of the name Christian. Thus, one might want to say *more* than we will say here, or to say it in a different way, but Christians are committed to at least this much.

For all Christians, salvation is a gift from God that is connected to the ultimate ends or purposes for which God created us. Whatever else and however else Christians speak of these matters, they all affirm that God created us for communion, fellowship, and friendship with the Father, Son, Holy Spirit, and each other. We are, so to speak, created for life with God, to become part of the Trinitarian family.

If this is why God created us, then salvation involves being brought to that goal. It is also true that because of our sin, we cannot reach this goal on our own. If we are to reach it, we will need God's help. God's help is revealed to us decisively in the life, death, and resurrection of Jesus Christ. Interestingly, scripture itself narrates for us the scope and nature of God's desires for us, the extent to which our sin frustrates those desires, Christ's decisive intervention on our behalf, and the ways we are to live together in the light of that intervention.

Said another way, Christians recognize that scripture is one of the gifts God gives us to fulfill God's desire to bring us to salvation. As we read, engage, and ultimately embody the words of scripture, God brings us to our proper end or goal in Christ. In this respect, scripture is an instrument of God's will to save us. Along these same lines, Saint Augustine in the fifth century speaks of scripture as a vehicle which carries us to our true home along the road created by Christ.

Scripture is also unique among God's gifts in that it *both* plays a role in God's plan of reconciling all things in Christ (2 Corinthians 5:19) *and* it is the place where that plan is authoritatively and dramatically revealed. In fact, we Christians find ourselves in a happily circular pattern regarding our involvement with scripture and our lives with God. The pattern looks like this: A discerning understanding of God's work of salvation enables Christians to read and embody scripture in ways that allow God to draw us into our proper place in that work. We might think of this as being given a part in a drama and provided with a script from the director. Rightly inhabiting our place in God's drama of salvation allows us to perceive the movements of that drama more clearly. This enables us to understand scripture better. A better, deeper understanding of scripture draws us into ever deeper friendship with God and with others. So it goes until this drama is brought to its conclusion.

Knowing the contours and movements of God's drama of salvation will help us both to understand scripture better and to take our place in that drama more fully. In this light, the aim of this study is to introduce you to this drama of salvation as it is laid out in scripture. Over the next several weeks you will examine the drama's central episodes. You will also explore some of the passages in scripture where these episodes are most clearly displayed. Part of the hope of this book is that your congregation will come away with some common language for navigating sometimes challenging conversations about these key ideas.

It is also important to recognize that there are other alternative ways or frameworks for understanding scripture. This has been true from the very beginning of Christianity. Some of these ways are problematic. That is, they present the drama of salvation in ways that ignore or deform important aspects of Christianity. For example, some early readers of scripture found an account of two Gods, the God of the Jews and the divine character, Jesus. Indeed, they found the passion accounts indicated that God and Jesus were enemies. They assimilated those two gods into the vast variety of gods characteristic of Greco-Roman polytheism, which included such divine and quasi-divine figures as Nebro, Saklas, Harmozel, and the 365 Archontes. Once this happened, it was fairly easy for these interpreters of scripture to absorb and transform Christian views into the dominant philosophical and cultural viewpoints of the day. Christianity became one more form of philosophical speculation; certainly not something one might die for.

This may sound like a story from another galaxy, but it all happened in the second century. We know these readers of scripture as Gnostics, and they represented a very powerful challenge to Christian faith and practice. The only way to counter this way of reading scripture was to have an alternative framework that maintained the integrity of Christianity. If you want to read more of this framework you can look at Irenaeus of Lyon's book, *Against Heresies*.

Although we may not be tempted by this particular form of Gnosticism, it is often easy for Christians to interpret scripture in ways that end up assimilating Christianity into one of the dominant philosophies or ideologies of our day, whether it be nationalism or consumerism or white supremacy.

This is just one brief example of an inappropriate framework for reading scripture. There are also many different ways to present this drama that neither assimilate Christianity into some other collection of beliefs and practices nor require a substantial reformulation of Christian doctrine. These different frameworks are not in direct competition with each other. They can exist happily side by side. What is presented here is but one framework that can accommodate the different contours of Christian convictions.

When it comes to discerning the differences between appropriate and inappropriate frameworks; when it comes to thinking about which appropriate framework best suits the needs of specific contexts; those who are already proficient readers and practitioners of scripture are best equipped to succeed. The better we read, mark, learn, and inwardly digest scripture, the better we will be able to evaluate and employ different ways of presenting the scope or framework of scripture.

Before getting into the heart of things, it will be important to make a significant distinction. Throughout these studies, you will read references to "Israel." Where you read this, please understand that this is a reference to ancient Israel as a central figure in the Old Testament. In this case, "Israel" refers to the people of God; the children of Abraham, Sarah, Rebekah, Isaac, Jacob, and their descendants. As you read their stories you will read about great faith, righteous deeds, stunning failures, deceptions, frauds, odd family dynamics, and so forth. These are people like us. At the same time, you will also be aware that there exists today a nation state called Israel. Whether and how biblical Israel is connected to modern-day Israel is a complex and contested matter. There is room for honest disagreements among Christians about such connections. Without entering into those matters, we should note that nothing said in these studies about biblical Israel is offered with the idea that it would also apply to modern-day Israel.

Throughout this study we will use the term "Old Testament" to refer to the first part of the Christian Bible. Some people use the term "Hebrew Bible" to refer to these books. This is typically an attempt to describe this set of books in more neutral terms. The phrase "Old Testament" can convey the sense of being outdated or inferior relative to the "New Testament." In addition, these books are not the "Old Testament" for Jews; they are simply the Bible, or the "Tanakh" (a Hebrew term for the three parts of the Jewish scripture). In the light of subsequent Christian violence against Jews, a phrase like "Old Testament" might imply an anti-Jewish bias.

Both of these are serious concerns. Christians must remember they cannot rightly understand the New Testament without the Old. The Old Testament is neither inferior to nor eliminated by the presence of the New. Both are indispensable parts of the Christian Bible. Referring to this set of writings as the Old Testament reminds us that we are reading this set of Jewish books *as Christians*.

Although the term "Hebrew Bible" is an attempt to avoid the two concerns named above, it also has some difficulties. While the Old Testament books were written in Hebrew, almost all contemporary Christians read these texts in translation and not Hebrew. Indeed, the vast majority of first century Christians and many Jews read or listened to the Old Testament in its Greek translation (the Septuagint) rather than in Hebrew. Again, while granting the integrity of Judaism, Christians must also recognize that Jews and Christians approach the texts that Christians call the Old Testament in very different ways, ways that are potentially obscured by the use of a phrase like "Hebrew Bible."

You may well have already done some study of the Bible as a whole. This study may be different in that it will not take you through each book individually, introducing you to themes and data related to each book of the Bible. The objectives of these studies are somewhat different:

Objectives of this study as a whole

1. This study aims to help you develop an organizing framework for approaching scripture.

2. This framework will help fit the various pieces of Christian doctrine together in a way that is both scriptural and faithful to the central beliefs and practices of Christianity.

3. This study will provide you with the opportunity to discuss central features of scripture with fellow believers from your congregation.

4. This study invites you to see yourself as a participant in the ongoing drama of salvation as revealed in scripture.

5. This study will allow you to reflect on ways in which your congregational life fits into and helps you better understand both individual episodes in God's drama of salvation and the shape of scripture as a whole.

Planning and Organization

The following five points will explain how this material is organized into specific chapters and how each chapter might be approached in group settings. It is crucial to recognize, however, that this curriculum will not teach itself. This material presumes that the groups using it have been graced by the Holy Spirit with one or more wise leaders who can use this material in their own ministry as teachers within Christ's body. These materials cannot stand on their own as a substitute for such leadership.

1. Each chapter begins with a prayer designed to direct your thoughts and hearts toward the theme under discussion. Some of those prayers, as well as some of the prayers that conclude chapters, have been adapted by me to better fit their context.

2. Each study begins with some comments to help set the scene for that particular study. These can be read in advance or together as a group.

3. Participants will read passages of scripture that help to illustrate a particular episode in the drama of salvation.

THE FORM OF THE WORD

4. Participants can then be invited as a group to discuss specific questions related to the reading and to your personal and congregational life with God.

5. Each chapter will close with prayer.

Groups may want to enlarge upon or rearrange some of these elements in the light of their particular needs and experiences.

Norms

It is always helpful to reaffirm how we listen, talk, and interact with one another as we engage in Bible study. The following norms are invaluable in shaping a communal study process. As a group you may want to add to the list. Let us declare that it is okay to:

1. Participate in determining when and where the group will gather and then support the group through responsible attendance and participation.

2. Take responsibility for our own learning: Feel free to ask questions when confused and to make contributions when inspired.

3. Share and test our ideas with the group even before they are fully developed, so that others will be encouraged to share their thoughts as well.

4. Question the ideas being proposed in the group or in this study material but also question our own ideas and assumptions.

5. Treat this study as a wonderful and unique opportunity for spiritual growth, as a chance to think and pray together, and to clarify thoughts about who we are as the church.

6. Practice our best active listening skills; to be open and receptive to others.

7. Build on the ideas of others in the group to help ideas stretch and grow.

8. Expect that while we will learn personally, we will also learn and grow as a group.

Chapter One

Fitting Scripture's Pieces within a Framework

Opening Prayer

Blessed Lord, who caused all holy scriptures to be written for our learning: Help us so to hear them, read, mark, learn, and inwardly digest them, that we may embrace and ever hold fast the blessed hope of everlasting life, which you have given us in our Savior Jesus Christ; who lives and reigns with you and the Holy Spirit, one God, for ever and ever.

Proper 28
Book of Common Prayer

Perhaps you have been reading scripture for years; you know studying the Word of God brings both comfort and challenge. Or perhaps you may have tried to develop a habit of scripture study only to struggle with the many complexities of the Bible. Be assured, you are not the first to struggle this way. Even the first followers of Jesus had to grapple with how to understand how the life and death of Jesus fit into their understanding of scripture (which, for them, would have been the Old Testament). It was only after the resurrection that Christ "opened their minds to understand the scripture," (Luke 24:45). These Jewish disciples of Jesus, for whom the Old Testament was the only Bible they knew, came to see those texts anew in the light of the resurrected Christ. The resurrection provided the key that enabled them to fit the pieces of the Old Testament together in a new and unanticipated way. Of course, this new understanding did not emerge for them immediately. It developed over time as they were guided by the Spirit to a new and deeper understanding of the life, death, and resurrection of Jesus. In this way they developed a new framework for approaching scripture. They were able to see old, familiar verses in new and life-changing ways.

Read: Acts 8:26-40

Then an angel of the Lord said to Philip, "Get up and go toward the south to the road that goes down from Jerusalem to Gaza." (This is a wilderness road.) So he got up and went. Now there was an Ethiopian eunuch, a court official of the Candace, the queen of the Ethiopians, in charge of her entire treasury. He had come to Jerusalem to worship and was returning home; seated in his chariot, he was reading the prophet Isaiah. Then the Spirit said to Philip, "Go over to this chariot and join it." So Philip ran up to it and heard him reading the prophet Isaiah. He asked, "Do you understand what you are reading?" He replied, "How can I, unless someone guides me?" And he invited Philip to get in and sit beside him. Now the passage of the scripture that he was reading was this:

"Like a sheep he was led to the slaughter,
and like a lamb silent before its shearer,
so he does not open his mouth.
In his humiliation justice was denied him.
Who can describe his generation?
For his life is taken away from the earth."

The eunuch asked Philip, "About whom, may I ask you, does the prophet say this, about himself or about someone else?" Then Philip began to speak, and starting with this scripture he proclaimed to him the good news about Jesus. As they were going along the road, they came to some water, and the eunuch said, "Look, here is water! What is to prevent me from being baptized?" He commanded the chariot to stop, and both of them, Philip and the eunuch, went down into the water, and Philip baptized him. When they came up out of the water, the Spirit of the Lord snatched Philip away;

the eunuch saw him no more and went on his way rejoicing. But Philip found himself at Azotus, and as he was passing through the region he proclaimed the good news to all the towns until he came to Caesarea.

Questions to Ponder

1. What is at the root of the Ethiopian's struggle to understand scripture?

2. What does he need?

3. How does Philip open the scripture to the Ethiopian?

4. Have you ever had a moment when someone else (either in person or through something written) has helped open up a confusing passage to you? If so, please share some of that experience with your group. These moments help reinforce for us the truth that scripture is best read together as part of our common life together in Christ.

Setting the Scene

The example of Acts 8 provides us with a story where a biblical character, Philip, makes use of his beliefs about Jesus to look back on an Old Testament text in a new light. Here is another exercise related to the importance of fitting scripture within a framework.

This time it involves the question of how our predecessors in the faith held together crucial and essential claims from the Old Testament and the New Testament.

From the very beginnings of the church Christians have maintained that the Old Testament is just as much a part of scripture as the New Testament. Indeed, it was the only scripture Jesus, Paul, and Peter knew. Because they all treated the Old Testament as scripture, how could those who came after them do differently?

In the multicultural and religiously plural world of the first century, Jews stood out from all other groups for their commitment to the singularity of God. There was one God; all others were simply pretenders to be avoided.

The first followers of Jesus were all Jews and shared this commitment to the one God of Israel. Even as more and more non-Jews joined the church, the church retained its commitment to the Old Testament and its unrelenting insistence that there is only one God worthy of their love and worship. These Christians also asserted that Jesus Christ was God. They did not believe that Jesus became God, somehow gaining a promotion through his death and resurrection. Rather, Jesus, they believed, was always God (as John 1 and Philippians 2:5-11 assert).

Jesus is God; there is only one God (the God whom Jesus calls "Father" in the gospels). The Bible is unflinching in asserting both of these things without explaining how to hold these two (seemingly incompatible) assertions together. What is required, and what the later doctrine of the Trinity provides, is a more developed, scripturally regulated framework that allows Christians to assert both divine singularity and to locate Christ fully within God's singular identity. For most Christians, the doctrine of the Trinity can seem like a very confusing set of assertions that may be fascinating to theologians but really make no difference to everyday life. But I hope this book and the scriptural texts it examines will help us see that the doctrine of the Trinity, hammered out in the third and fourth centuries, *is* the appropriate framework for ordering Christians' scriptural claims about God. The identity of the one God of Israel is constituted by a trinity of persons (Father, Son, and Holy Spirit), distinct yet undivided. Without this framework Christians would have no obvious way both to worship the one God of Israel and to worship Jesus Christ as Lord.

Read: Exodus 20:1-5

Then God spoke all these words,

"I am the Lord your God, who brought you out of the land of Egypt, out of the house of slavery; you shall have no other gods before me. You shall not make for yourself an idol, whether in the form of anything that is in heaven above or that is on the earth beneath

or that is in the water under the earth. You shall not bow down to them or serve them, for I the Lord your God am a jealous God, punishing children for the iniquity of parents to the third and the fourth generation of those who reject me...

Additional Reading:
Deuteronomy 6:4-5; Isaiah 42:8

Questions to Ponder

1. What do you take to be the most significant claims these texts make about God?

2. What qualities or characteristics are attributed to God in these passages?

Read: John 1:1-5

In the beginning was the Word, and the Word was with God, and the Word was God. He was in the beginning with God. All things came into being through him, and without him not one thing came into being. What has come into being in him was life, and the life was the light of all people. The light shines in the darkness, and the darkness did not overtake it.

Additional Reading:
Philippians 2:6-11; Hebrews 1:1-4

Questions to Ponder

1. What do you take to be the most significant claims these texts make about Christ?

2. How is the relationship between Jesus and God talked about in these passages?

3. Do you see a conflict between the Old Testament's claims about God and the New Testament's claims about Christ? If so, how would you describe that conflict? How might you begin to resolve it?

4. Are there special phrases or activities in your worship or other aspects of your congregation's life where you are reminded of the Trinity?

Closing Prayer

Almighty God, who has revealed to your church your eternal Being of glorious majesty and perfect love as one God in Trinity of Persons: Give us grace to continue steadfast in the confession of this faith, and constant in our worship of you, Father, Son, and Holy Spirit; for you live and reign, one God, now and forever.

Amen.

Preface of Trinity Sunday
Book of Common Prayer

Chapter Two
The Beginning

Opening Prayer

Sovereign over all things, we acknowledge this universe was made for good, yet we tremble when vast systems shift and crumble despite our efforts to control them. Forgive our vain attempts to turn your gracious order to our profit and victory. Guide us in the ways of peace and reconciliation that we may enter into your unending and joyful reign.

Web of Creation

Setting the Scene

In the introduction, I briefly explored the notion that we were created for communion, fellowship, or friendship with God. These are all terms the Christian tradition has used to summarize God's purposes and deepest desires for creation. Each of these terms, however, really stands as a sort of summary of texts in the Bible that describe much more richly and dramatically the ends for which God created us.

When we turn to scripture for an account of God's purposes and desires for us, it is natural to start at the beginning: Genesis. In this chapter, we will do just that. In the next chapter, we will look at various accounts of the end of things to see how they develop and broaden our understanding of God's purposes and desires for us.

Before starting, we should note that many churches, locales, and even denominations may be caught up in fights over evolution and creationism. This study is not directly concerned with those issues. Long before the Scopes trial, St. Augustine (in the 5th century) indicated that Christians probably should not hold views about creation that put them irreconcilably at odds with the best science of their day. Augustine adopted this posture because to understand certain verses in Genesis well, one needs to recognize that they assert *that* God created all things and *why* God created all things. These verses are not primarily interested in *how* God created. When science tries to answer the "who" and "why" questions it may be saying more than the evidence warrants. When Christians use Genesis to answer the "how" question, they may be asserting more than these texts do.

Although it is possible to argue that the creation of humans in the image of God is the climactic moment of creation (Genesis 1:26-27), we would do well to focus on the seventh day as the climax of creation. It is there that we learn why and for what purpose God created. The seventh day is the day of rest. Unlike the other six days, it never ends. There is no evening and morning (Genesis 2:1–3). Thus, the seventh day both marks the end of God's creative activity and indicates the purpose for which God creates. God created us for rest. This is not to say that the couch potato is the godliest form of life! Instead, when we say that God created us for rest, we need to take our cues from the subsequent description of life in the Garden.

First, think of the relationship between God and humans. God is said to walk in the Garden in the cool of the day (3:8). God converses with the humans face to face, as it were. These are images of extraordinary intimacy between God and humans. God and humans enjoy unbroken community and communication. In addition, the humans do not have to struggle to find food and water. Creation is bountiful. The humans do not have to protect themselves from the elements. Humans do not have to fear the animals and the animals do not fear the humans. God, humans, and creation are all in their proper relationship to others and themselves. Right relationship between God, humans, and the rest of the created world is at the heart of the Hebrew word *shalom,* or peace. When we say that God's purpose in creating is that all things should enjoy rest, the rest of the seventh day, we mean that God desires us to live in *shalom*.

To understand this idea better, it may help to think in terms of the Sabbath. The Hebrew word for seven is *shabbat*. The sabbath or *shabbat* simply refers to the seventh day. If you know observant Jews and have seen their sabbath practices, you get a little sense of the rest for which God created us. All of the work and anxieties of the week are put aside. The day is devoted, on the one hand, to study, prayer and restful contemplation of God and, on the other, to enjoyment of family and friends.

Of course, the peaceable rest of creation does not last long, as Genesis 3-11 makes clear. We will look at that soon. At this point is it sufficient to recognize that God's purpose in creation, God's deepest desire for us, is peaceable rest, a perfect Sabbath.

Read: Genesis 1:26-31

Then God said, "Let us make humans in our image, according to our likeness, and let them have dominion over the fish of the sea and over the birds of the air and over the cattle and over all the wild animals of the earth and over every creeping thing that creeps upon the earth."

*So God created humans in his image,
in the image of God he created them;
male and female he created them.*

God blessed them, and God said to them, "Be fruitful and multiply and fill the earth and subdue it and have dominion over the fish of the sea and over the birds of the air and over every living thing that moves upon the earth." God said, "See, I have given you every plant yielding seed that is upon the face of all the earth and every tree with seed in its fruit; you shall have them for food. And to every beast of the earth and to every bird of the air and to everything that creeps on the earth, everything that has the breath of life, I have given every green plant for food." And it was so. God saw everything that he had made, and indeed, it was very good. And there was evening and there was morning, the sixth day.

Additional Reading: Genesis 1:1-25; Genesis 2

Questions to Ponder

1. Creation is repeatedly characterized as "good." What does this tell us about God? What does this tell us about creation?

2. How would you characterize the relationship between God and the first man and woman? Does that tell you anything about God's deepest desires for humans?

3. God peaceably provides for the needs of the first humans. What might that tell you about God's desires for humans?

4. What aspects of your congregation's life and worship help you to understand and enjoy the rest God wants for us?

5. Are there aspects of your life or your congregation's life that keep you from enjoying God's *shalom*? Explain.

Closing Prayer

Living God, we are beset on many sides by distractions and detractors: those who would have us place our hope in appearances, in wealth and power. Help us to keep you in the center of our sight, that we may hold fast to what is life giving, and live in your grace.

Web of Creation

Chapter Three

The End is the Beginning

Opening Prayer

O Lord our God, splendor and honor and power are yours by right. You have created all things, and by your will they exist and have their being; O Lamb that was slain, with your blood you have redeemed for God, from every family and language, people and nation, a kingdom of priests to serve our God. To him who sits on the throne, and to Christ the Lamb, be worship and praise, dominion and splendor, forever and for evermore.

Amen.

Adapted from Revelation 4:11; 5:9-10, 13

Setting the Scene

In the previous chapter, we looked at God's deepest desires for humanity as revealed in Genesis 1-2. If you know much about Genesis, you know the peaceable and harmonious *shalom* for which God created us does not last very long. Indeed, one could read Genesis 3-11 as the story of how humanity becomes ever more captivated by violence, power, and domination (see Genesis 6:11-13).

God's desires for us, however, do not change. In this chapter, we will look at several passages that reflect on the way things will look at the end of time, when the redemption of the world is at hand. Even though the contexts and the images have changed, these passages, nevertheless, make it plain that God's deepest desires for humanity, as displayed in the garden, will ultimately be brought to fruition.

One place we see this is in the prophets. If you are familiar with prophetic writings, you know that they are filled with long passages describing the sin, oppression, and injustice that mark the life of the people of God. They also anticipate God's coming judgment. What is sometimes less well known is that despite this coming judgment, the prophets also speak to God's coming redemption.

One of the fullest accounts of God's coming redemption, however, comes at the very end of the Bible, at the end of the book of Revelation. In Revelation we see that what begins in a garden ends in a city, the New Jerusalem. If you look at the central sets of relationships in the Garden—God and humans; God and creation; humans and creation; and humans with each other—it is clear that the New Jerusalem described in Revelation brings God's deepest desires for humanity as seen in creation to fruition, restoring everything to its proper relationship to God, itself and to others.

The intimacy between God and humans is restored. Instead of walking in the garden and speaking with the humans face to face, Revelation 21:3 indicates that God will dwell with humans, "God himself will be with them." There is no significant distance between God and humans and no need for sacrifices (see verse 22: "I saw no temple in the city for its temple is the Lord, the Almighty and the Lamb,"). The damage brought into the world through human skin is healed (22:2). Despair, sadness, and death are all defeated and the shalom of the garden is restored. The city has walls and gates, but these are not for protection and security. Rather, they are there simply for beauty's sake to adorn the city properly. In fact, the gates are always open. Peace between nations is established and all the world now gives glory to the Lord.

Although the idiom or setting has shifted from a garden to a city, God's deepest intentions and purposes for humanity and the world are completed here in the New Jerusalem. Of course, a great deal takes place between Genesis 1-2 and Revelation 21-22. The remainder of our chapters will present one way of filling in the events that come between creation and redemption. The aim will not be to touch on every single episode of significance; instead, we will try to illustrate some of the larger movements of the drama. As you begin to internalize the grand scope of scripture you will start to develop a sense of how any biblical passage you might study can be fitted into this drama. One of the chief goals of *The Form of the Word* is to help you learn how to fit both your reading of scripture and the shape of your own life and the life of your congregation into this drama.

Read: Isaiah 2:1-4

The word that Isaiah son of Amoz saw concerning Judah and Jerusalem.

In days to come
the mountain of the Lord's house
shall be established as the highest of the mountains
and shall be raised above the hills;
all the nations shall stream to it.
Many peoples shall come and say,

"Come, let us go up to the mountain of the Lord,
to the house of the God of Jacob,
that he may teach us his ways
and that we may walk in his paths."
For out of Zion shall go forth instruction
and the word of the Lord from Jerusalem.
He shall judge between the nations
and shall arbitrate for many peoples;
they shall beat their swords into plowshares
and their spears into pruning hooks;
nation shall not lift up sword against nation;
neither shall they learn war any more.

Additional Reading: Isaiah 65:17-25; Amos 9:11-15; Revelation 21-22:5

Questions to Ponder

1. Based on these passages, what will be some of the main characteristics of the world when it is redeemed?

2. Do you find any foretastes of this coming redemption in your own life and experiences? Be specific!

3. Are there any aspects of your congregational life and worship that provide foretastes of this coming redemption? Be specific with examples.

4. Do these accounts of God's redemption make any difference to the way you and/or your congregation live in the world today? How so?

Closing Prayer

O Ruler of the universe, Lord God: Great are the deeds you have done, surpassing human understanding. Your ways are always righteous and true, O ruler of the ages. Who can fail to pay you homage, Lord, and sing the praises of your holy Name? Only you are the Holy One. All nations will draw near and fall down before you, because you are just and your holy works have been revealed. Glory to the Father, and to the Son and to the Holy Spirit: as it was in the beginning, is now, and will be forever.

Amen.

Adapted from Revelation 15:3-4

Chapter Four
The Call of Abraham

Opening Prayer

Steer the ship of our lives, good Lord, to your quiet harbor, where we can be safe from the storms of sin and conflict. Show us the course we should take. Renew in us the gift of discernment, so that we can always see the direction in which we should go. And give us the strength and the courage to choose the right course, even when the sea is rough and the waves are high, knowing that through enduring hardship and danger in your name we shall find comfort and peace.

Adapted from Basil of Caesarea

Setting the Scene

The heavenly city of the book of Revelation is not nameless, but neither is it called the city of God. It is the New Jerusalem, recalling the name of a city that already existed.

Jerusalem and its Temple were the center of worship for the people of Israel, the Jews. The New Jerusalem links the redemption of the world to God's relationship with a particular people. In this chapter we will begin to explore the significance of this, and we must begin with Abraham.

The story of Abraham and his family begins in Genesis 12. You will recall that the *shalom* of the Garden is broken by human sin. The humans disobey God, eat from the forbidden tree, and are expelled from the Garden (Genesis 3). Because of Adam's and Eve's sin, they are alienated from God; they are also alienated from creation and forced to struggle in order to survive. Additionally, humans are alienated from each other. For example, in Genesis 4 we read about the first murder. From this point on we get a picture of a world increasingly marked by violence and vengeance. By the time we get to Genesis 6, the world "is corrupt and filled with violence" (6:11). The world now exemplifies the very antithesis of the peace for which God created it.

In the light of human violence, God sends a great flood. On the one hand, there is clearly a need for some sort of purge and renewal of creation. On the other hand, if God were simply to eliminate everything and start again from scratch, it would mean that humans were capable of ultimately undermining God's desires for creation. The flood allows both a cleansing and renewal of creation (Genesis 7:11-2; 8:17; and 9:7 use language that draws directly from Genesis 1-2), yet it also retains continuity with the world God initially made.

Noah and his family are not long out of the Ark before things start to go wrong again. Genesis 9:18-28 very delicately relates what appears to be an act of sexual violence. Through the line of one of Noah's sons, Ham, we meet Nimrod, the founder of the city of Babel (10:10). Although there seems to be a newfound solidarity among humans, it is solidarity based on pride and fear (11:1-4). It comes as no great surprise that God acts to separate these people from each other. Things seem poised to relapse into violence when we are introduced to Abraham.

In Genesis 4-11, God addresses the brokenness of creation and the scope of human violence in a grand way. God seems to shift gears in Genesis 12 to focus on one person, Abraham. There are two important things to recognize about Abraham. First, nothing about Abraham makes him worthy of God's choice. Indeed, the first words he speaks in Genesis are about conspiring with his wife to lie about her status in order to save his life (see 13:11-13). God's choice of Abraham is simply that: God's gracious choice. Yes, Abraham believes God and follows. He grows into a man of great faith and faithfulness, but that is not how God finds him initially. The importance of this focus on God's choice and not Abraham's becomes clear when we recognize that the aim of God's choosing of Abraham is to bring a blessing to all the families of the earth (12:3). God opts to bless this one man and his heirs as part of God's plan to bring a blessing to all the nations and thus to bring about God's best intentions for creation. That is, the choosing of Abraham is God's choice to bless all of creation.

If Abraham's faith or righteousness made him worthy of God's choice, then we would have to be equally worthy to participate in God's blessing. Instead, when God calls Abraham, he is just like us. As Paul will note later on (Romans 4:1-25), we, Gentiles and Jews, participate in the blessings promised to Abraham through faith, just as "Abraham believed God and it was reckoned to him as righteousness" (Genesis 15:6). Abraham was not righteous in advance of this blessing.

The precise shape of God's blessing of Abraham is made clear in the covenant God makes with Abraham. This covenant is presented most fully in Genesis 17. We should note several crucial characteristics of this covenant: First, this covenant is "everlasting" (17:7). There is nothing Abraham did to earn this blessing and there is nothing he or his heirs can do to revoke it. God is willingly, graciously bound to Abraham and his heirs forever. More concretely, God promises Abraham descendants and bountiful land. Regardless of how these concrete promises may have become wrapped up in contemporary geopolitics, land and descendants are the basic ingredients for stability and flourishing. Much of Genesis through Joshua can be read as the story of God bringing these promises to fruition. In addition, God promises, "to be God to you and your offspring after you," (Genesis 17:7-8). This is a promise of God's faithful abiding presence across time and place. This promise is reiterated in the resurrected Christ's promise at the end of Matthew, "I will be with you always, even to the end of the age" (Matthew 28:20).

In making these promises, God would appear to be laying out the course of events for much of the rest of scripture. In one sense this is true. In another sense, however, it becomes clear that God's plans for the ways things should unfold often takes humans by surprise. As Genesis unfolds, we will see that once Abraham and his family are given these promises, they immediately begin to try to manipulate situations to make the promises come true. This results in a sometimes horrific, sometimes comical interplay between humans' attempts to bring about God's promises and God's own working to fulfill the covenant. Think of the terrifying account of Hagar and Ishmael (Genesis 16; 21:8-20) as well as the comic account of how Isaac and Rebekah each tries to ensure that their favored son receives Isaac's blessing (Genesis 27:1-40).

If our notions of equality lead us to be offended by God's selectivity in choosing Abraham, it may be important to remember that the calling of Abraham and formation of a chosen people, Israel, are part of God's plan to bring a blessing to *all* the families of the earth (Genesis 12:3). God chooses Israel so that the relationship between God and the people of Israel is to be so beautiful, fascinating, and compelling that it will draw all the nations to God.

One final note

Christians only need to observe the world around them to see that these promises to Abraham have a capacity to be taken up in diverse ways. For example, Jews and Christians each see themselves as heirs of God's promises to Abraham—sometimes to the exclusion of the other group. On top of that, some Jews and some Christians see the presence of the modern nation-state of Israel as a concrete fulfillment of those promises to Abraham. Others think the connections between Israel in scripture and modern Israel are contested and complex. They magnify the differences between these two Israels rather than similarities.

Conversation about these matters is further complicated by the long history of Christian violence against Jews, climaxing in Christian complicity in the Holocaust. On top of this violence, the ways in which the modern nation-state of Israel has treated Palestinians (many of whom are Christians) further divides Jews and Christians.

Your congregation may be quite united in its viewpoints. Others may be sharply divided. Many congregations will find just getting conversations about this off the ground provokes intense emotion and disagreement. If your congregation is not well practiced at sustaining difficult conversations and debates along with the practices of confession, forgiveness, and reconciliation that necessarily accompany such conversations, it might be best to exercise caution and care about diving into this issue too deeply.

All of this is to say, for the purposes of thinking about the shape of scripture, these studies focus on Israel as a scriptural entity tied to the promises made to Abraham and his kin.

Read: Genesis 12:1-3

Now the Lord said to Abram, "Go from your country and your kindred and your father's house to the land that I will show you. I will make of you a great nation, and I will bless you and make your name great, so that you will be a blessing. I will bless those who bless you, and the one who curses you I will curse, and in you all the families of the earth shall be blessed."

Additional Reading:
Genesis 17:1-15; Galatians 3:6-9, 27-29

Questions to Ponder

1. Of all the possible people to call, why do you think God calls Abraham?

2. What is the ultimate aim of this call?

3. How would you define a covenant? What are the characteristics of this particular covenant?

4. What does God promise to Abraham? Be specific in your answer. What are Abraham's responsibilities as a covenantal partner with God?

5. Can you see ways in which this covenant helps advance the aims for which God first called Abraham? Explain.

6. If God's covenant with Abraham is "everlasting," how do we as Christians fit into that covenant?

Closing Prayer

Sing to the Lord a new song;
Sing to the Lord, all the whole earth.

Sing to the Lord and bless his Name;
Proclaim the good news of his salvation from day to day.

Declare his glory among the nations and his wonders among all the peoples. Ascribe to the Lord, O families of the peoples, Ascribe to the Lord glory and strength.

Ascribe to the Lord the glory due his name; bring an offering, and come into his courts. Worship the Lord in holy splendor; tremble before him, all the earth.

Psalm 96:1-3; 7-9

Chapter Five

A People

Opening Prayer

Let us sing to the LORD for he has triumphed gloriously; horse and rider he has thrown into the sea. The LORD is my strength and my might and he has become my salvation; this is my God, and I will praise him, my father's God and I will exalt him. The LORD is a warrior; the LORD is his name.

Adapted from Exodus 15:1-3

Setting the Scene

God's covenant with Abraham includes three central promises: numerous descendants, land, and to be their God forever. The rest of Genesis can be seen as a series of attempts by the book's main characters to bring the first of God's promises to fruition. At the same time, these human efforts are often frustrated, altered, or transformed by a God who works in unexpected and unpredictable ways to sustain the promises of the covenant. For example, contrary to custom and expectation, God works through the younger son in order to multiply Abraham's descendants (Isaac and Jacob are both second sons, Joseph is the 11th of 12). Despite the human scheming, jealousy, and deception that marks much of Genesis 12-50, God preserves and multiplies the heirs of Abraham. At the end of Genesis, when Joseph finally has a chance to exact revenge upon his brothers for all they had done to him he offers mercy instead. He summarizes this central theme of Genesis when he notes, "Even though you intended to do harm to me, God intended it for good, in order to preserve a numerous people as he is doing today," (50:20).

By the end of Genesis, the people of Israel are both numerous and prosperous. They are not, however, in the land God promised to give them. Rather, they are in Egypt where they enjoy a special status because of Joseph's special status. At the beginning of Exodus, we read an ominous verse: "Now a new king arose over Egypt who did not know Joseph," (Exodus 1:8). This new king or Pharaoh apparently does not recognize the debts and obligations he owes to Joseph and Joseph's people. He views the Israelites as a large and potentially unstable alien population in the midst of Egypt. In Pharaoh's eyes, the Israelites have become a threat to Egypt's stability. He attempts to deal with this by enslaving the Israelites and trying to exterminate them.

God steps into this situation to rescue the Israelites from destruction and to lead them into the Promised Land. Exodus contains many significant elements, but for our purposes, three revelations are particularly important: God's name to Moses and to the people, God's powerful deeds on behalf of Israel, and God's love and care for Israel in giving the law.

In Exodus 3, God appears to Moses in the form of a burning bush. God calls Moses to return to Egypt and lead the Israelites out from slavery and genocide into the land God originally promised to Abraham. Moses is quite reluctant to take on this call. In 3:13-15, he speculates that the Israelites will want to know the name of this God who is calling them out of slavery and wants to know the name he should use when he speaks to them about God. God responds by revealing a name composed of four Hebrew letters. Hence, this name is sometimes referred to as the *tetragrammaton* (Greek for "four letters"). Because human lips are sinful, Jews do not pronounce this name. This name seems to be connected to the verb *to be* (hence the phrase, "I am who I am," in 3:14). Modern scholars often use the English designation, *Yahweh,* to refer to this name (adding vowels to aid in pronunciation). Most English translations of the Bible will use the word LORD in large or small caps to indicate the original Hebrew four-letter name of God. Both Judaism and Christianity contain a rich literary tradition reflecting on and contemplating the various aspects of God's name. For our purposes, this name, Yahweh, provides a distinct identity for the God of the Israelites: Yahweh is distinguishable from all the other named gods of the ancient world.

Indeed, one, but by no means the only, way to look at the first half of Exodus is as a battle between Pharaoh, the god-king of Egypt, and the LORD (Yahweh), the god of a ragtag group of slaves, led by a fugitive. When Moses first goes to Pharaoh and tells him the LORD has called the people out of Egypt and Pharaoh should let them go, Pharaoh replies, "Who is the LORD that I should heed him and let Israel go? I do not know the LORD and I will not let Israel go," (Exodus 5:2). Pharaoh, arguably the most powerful man on earth and a god in his own right, throws down the gauntlet in this verse. For the next ten chapters, through a series of mighty acts, the LORD displays a comprehensive mastery of and superiority to Pharaoh. This mastery is so complete that the LORD can even control Pharaoh's heart.

This aspect of the "hardening of Pharaoh's heart" often leads modern readers to pause and reflect on the justice of this act. Namely: Is it fair that God hardens Pharaoh's heart and then punishes him and his people for his hard heart? If the issue is put this way, within the context of a courtroom, it takes on a particular hue. Alternatively, in the context of the narrative of Exodus, it is important to recognize that the LORD hardens Pharaoh's heart after the sixth, eighth, ninth, and final plagues. The other times, we learn either that Pharaoh hardens his own heart or simply that his heart is hardened. The narrative builds to implicate Pharaoh much more directly in his own demise and the demise of his people. Moreover, this is a ruler who is perpetuating genocidal policies against the people of the LORD. One expects the LORD to act in response to this injustice. Recognition of these factors does not resolve all issues but should help us better understand the relationship between Pharaoh and the LORD.

When the law is first given to the people of Israel, it is significant that the commandments begin, "I am the LORD your god who brought you up out of the land of Egypt. You shall have no other gods before me," (Exodus 20:2–3). The giving of the law presumes God's mighty and even terrifying acts on behalf of Israel. The LORD reminds the Israelites that the LORD has spared nothing to redeem Israel. The LORD has displayed both great power and steadfast love. The commandments recall this steadfast love and provide the people of God with instructions about how to live with God, each other, and the world in order to keep that loving relationship in good working order.

In addition, by linking the commandments to God's deliverance of the Israelites, we are reminded that in settings such as Moses' and our own, where many gods vie for our time, attention, and allegiance, only the LORD is worthy of such a commitment from us. Redirecting our attention and affections away from the LORD is a basic goal of all types of idolatry. This is why idolatry is the central and most persistent threat to Israel's and the church's relationship with God. In chapter 8, we will look at idolatry and how it works to frustrate the drama of God's redemption of the world.

The Name of God

Read: Exodus 3:1-15

Moses was keeping the flock of his father-in-law Jethro, the priest of Midian; he led his flock beyond the wilderness and came to Mount Horeb, the mountain of God. There the angel of the Lord appeared to him in a flame of fire out of a bush; he looked, and the bush was blazing, yet it was not consumed. Then Moses said, "I must turn aside and look at this great sight and see why the bush is not burned up." When the Lord saw that he had turned aside to see, God called to him out of the bush, "Moses, Moses!" And he said, "Here I am." Then he said, "Come no closer! Remove the sandals from your feet, for the place on which you are standing is holy ground." He said further, "I am the God of your father, the God of Abraham, the God of Isaac, and the God of Jacob." And Moses hid his face, for he was afraid to look at God.

Then the Lord said, "I have observed the misery of my people who are in Egypt; I have heard their cry on account of their taskmasters. Indeed, I know their sufferings, and I have come down to deliver them from the Egyptians and to bring them up out of that land to a good and spacious land, to a land flowing with milk and honey, to the country of the Canaanites, the Hittites, the Amorites, the Perizzites, the Hivites, and the Jebusites. The cry of the Israelites has now come to me; I have also seen how the Egyptians oppress them. Now go, I am sending you to Pharaoh to bring my people, the Israelites, out of Egypt." But Moses said to God, "Who am I that I should go to Pharaoh and bring the Israelites out of Egypt?" He said, "I will be with you, and this shall be the sign for you that it is I who sent you: when you have brought the people out of Egypt, you shall serve God on this mountain."

But Moses said to God, "If I come to the Israelites and say to them, 'The God of your ancestors has sent me to you,' and they ask me, 'What is his name?' what shall I say to them?" God said to Moses, "I am who I am." He said further, "Thus you shall say to the Israelites, 'I am has sent me to you.'" God also said to Moses, "Thus you shall say to the Israelites, 'The Lord, the God of your ancestors, the God of Abraham, the God of Isaac, and the God of Jacob, has sent me to you:

*This is my name forever,
and this my title for all generations.*

Additional Reading: Deuteronomy 6:4-5

Questions to Ponder

1. Why do you think it was important for Moses to learn God's name? What other biblical stories have you encountered in which someone's name (or name change) was significant?

2. What does it mean—concretely, specifically—to love God with all your heart, soul, and mind? What aspects of your congregation's life and worship help you better love God in this way?

3. What makes it difficult to love God this way?

God's Mighty Acts

The passages below indicate what is most important for the Israelites to remember about God's actions in Exodus.

Read: Exodus 13:3-10

Moses said to the people, "Remember this day on which you came out of Egypt, out of the house of slavery, because the Lord brought you out from there by strength of hand; no leavened bread shall be eaten. Today, in the month of Abib, you are going out. When the Lord brings you into the land of the Canaanites, the Hittites, the Amorites, the Hivites, and the Jebusites, which he swore to your ancestors to give you, a land flowing with milk and honey, you shall keep this observance in this month. Seven days you shall eat unleavened bread, and on the seventh day there shall be a festival to the Lord. Unleavened bread shall be eaten for seven days; no leavened bread shall be seen in your possession, and no leaven shall be seen among you in all your territory. You shall tell your child on that day, 'It is because of what the Lord did for me when I came out of Egypt.' It shall serve for you as a sign on your hand and as a reminder on your forehead, so that the teaching of the Lord may be on your lips, for with a strong hand the Lord brought you out of Egypt. You shall keep this ordinance at its proper time from year to year.

Additional Reading:
Exodus 12:1-27; Deuteronomy 26:1-10

Questions to Ponder

1. What do these summaries tell you about God's actions?

2. If you were an Israelite, how do you think you'd feel when you read these passages? How might you feel if you were a regular everyday Egyptian?

3. What significance do these texts have for our life together as Christians?

The Commandments

Read: Exodus 20:1-17

Then God spoke all these words,

"I am the Lord your God, who brought you out of the land of Egypt, out of the house of slavery; you shall have no other gods before me. You shall not make for yourself an idol, whether in the form of anything that is in heaven above or that is on the earth beneath or that is in the water under the earth. You shall not bow down to them or serve them, for I the Lord your God am a jealous God, punishing children for the iniquity of parents to the third and the fourth generation of those who reject me but showing steadfast love to the thousandth generation of those who love me and keep my

commandments.

You shall not make wrongful use of the name of the Lord your God, for the Lord will not acquit anyone who misuses his name.

Remember the Sabbath day and keep it holy. Six days you shall labor and do all your work. But the seventh day is a Sabbath to the Lord your God; you shall not do any work—you, your son or your daughter, your male or female slave, your livestock, or the alien resident in your towns. For in six days the Lord made heaven and earth, the sea, and all that is in them, but rested the seventh day; therefore the Lord blessed the Sabbath day and consecrated it.

Honor your father and your mother, so that your days may be long in the land that the Lord your God is giving you.

You shall not murder.

You shall not commit adultery.

You shall not steal.

You shall not bear false witness against your neighbor.

You shall not covet your neighbor's house; you shall not covet your neighbor's wife, male or female slave, ox, donkey, or anything that belongs to your neighbor."

Questions to Ponder

1. Does it make a difference to your understanding of these commandments to see them in the context of all that has come before in Exodus? How so?

2. How would you describe the role of the Ten Commandments in the life of your congregation? (For example, does your congregation regularly read or recite the Ten Commandments? Are they ever alluded to? In what contexts?)

3. In light of the larger context of the commandments (God's covenant with Israel; the exodus event), what do you think about the display of the Ten Commandments in public places, like schools or courthouses?

4. Why do you think most people generally view the commandments as directed toward individuals rather than toward the community's life together?

5. Are there aspects of your congregation's life and worship that help you to focus your attention, time, and actions solely on God? Do you think it's possible to focus your attention, time, and actions solely on God all by yourself without community? Why or why not?

Closing Prayer

Happy are those whose way is blameless,
who walk in the law of the LORD.
Happy are those who keep his decrees,
who seek him with their whole heart,
who also do no wrong,
but walk in his ways.

You, Lord, have commanded your precepts
to be kept diligently.
O that our ways may be steadfast
in keeping your statutes!
Then we shall not be put to shame,
having our eyes fixed on all your commandments.

We will praise you with an upright heart,
when we learn your righteous ordinances.
We will observe your statutes;
do not forsake us.

Adapted from Psalm 119:1-8

Chapter Six
Land and Jubilee

Opening Prayer

Almighty and most merciful God, you command us to offer food to the hungry and to satisfy the needs of the afflicted. Through your holy and life-giving Spirit, direct every human heart, so that, following in the steps of your Son, we may give of ourselves in the service of others.

From The Episcopal Church's
"A Bidding Prayer to End Global Poverty"

Setting the scene

Eventually, the Israelites come to occupy the land God wants to give them. Readers will recognize several things at this point in the story: This land is already occupied; the Israelites have to fight to inhabit the land; the Israelites end up living among and side-by-side with the prior inhabitants. Sometimes this is a relatively benign situation, and sometimes it erupts into hostility. Throughout these texts, it is assumed that ultimately the land belongs to the LORD, who can give it or take it away. This reality should lead all contemporary Christians to exercise restraint in assuming they or the countries they inhabit are likewise called to occupy other places. The LORD's promise of land to the people of Abraham is not a model for the activities of modern nation states.

Even recognizing this distinction, it is important to see that the gift of the land is a difficult blessing to appreciate properly. The land is a concrete manifestation of God's care and faithfulness. The land also provides specific occasions for the Israelites to stumble in their walk with God and in their common life. For example, on the one hand, the land provides bountiful sustenance for the people. It is a land flowing with milk and honey (Exodus 3:18 and elsewhere). This bounty is clearly what God wants. On the other hand, the agricultural economy of the ancient world is very fragile. Pests, drought, storms, and marauding armies can ruin a harvest. In these cases, subsistence farmers begin a downward spiral into destitution and ultimately indentured servitude, as they are forced to sell their only asset, the land, in order to feed themselves and their families. As some slide into poverty, others may end up growing rich as they profit from the desperate circumstances of others. Such situations are the breeding grounds for the kinds of corruption and injustice denounced by the prophets.

Through a variety of laws and policies regarding indentured servitude and land ownership, it is clear that God does not intend long-running generational poverty. The most striking set of these laws and policies appear in Leviticus 25, with its description of the Jubilee year. The Jubilee year is a massive prescription for recalibrating the Israelites' economic life so that the poverty into which people can easily fall in an ancient agrarian economy does continue generation after generation. The premise that underwrites the Jubilee year is the notion that the land belongs to God, "The land shall not be sold in perpetuity, for the land is mine; with me you are but aliens and tenants," (Leviticus 25:23). By commanding the Israelites to observe the Jubilee, God reminds them that the land is not really theirs. More importantly, Jubilee prescribes the kind of life together that the Israelites are to embody so that they might properly serve as a light to the nations. The Jubilee commands indicate that the people are called to a life of dependence on God and each other, a life of generosity and sharing that keeps a light hold on individual possessions.

We do not know how and to what degree the Israelites observed the Jubilee year, if at all. It is easy to imagine that the powerful and rich, those who had the most to lose in this economic recalibration, would not have been eager to enact these commands.

For Christians, it is striking that when Jesus begins his first recorded preaching in Luke's gospel, he announces the "year of the Lord's favor," a reference to the Jubilee year that is being fulfilled in him (see Luke 4:16-30). The common life that God desires for Israel is given flesh and blood in the life and ministry of Jesus and those who follow him. Both in the book of Acts (especially chapters 4-5) and in some of Paul's letters (1 Corinthians 11:17-34), we see how the earliest Christians struggled with varying degrees of success to embody Jubilee in the particular contexts in which they found themselves. In our own world, Christians have invoked notions of the Jubilee to urge debt forgiveness for developing countries. All these examples are attempts to live in the light of the Jubilee presumptions that the land is God's, and we are tenants and aliens. God's provision of the land offers the blessing of sustenance and the invitation to a rich common life of sharing and generosity. This blessing brings with it the all too ready temptation to hoard and keep the land's blessings for oneself.

There is one more difficult blessing associated with God's giving of the land. This has to do with the sense of place and home that comes with the land. Think of how you feel when you return home after a long trip. Even if the trip were a wonderful vacation, it is always good to be home. Life in the Promised Land brings to an end the wandering that first began when God called Abraham to leave his home and family (Genesis 12). For Israel to live in the land is to be reminded daily of God's faithfulness. The land provides a very concrete way of participating in the intimacy that God desires to share with Israel and, through Israel, to share with all the nations.

It also becomes easy for Israel to assume that God feels just the way they do about living in the land. They even come to think that God sets up house in the land, ultimately coming to live in the Temple. Assuming God lives in the land with you brings with it the temptation to think you now have the world's best watch dog. The Israelites even begin to think, "God would never let anything bad happen to us in the land. God would never let anything happen to the Temple. It's God's house. Where would God go?" But God's commitment to the land, the city of Jerusalem, or the Temple is not like this. The prophets make it clear that unless they live well in the land, unless the Israelites "do justice, love kindness and walk humbly with God" (Micah 6:8), God will not let them remain in the land. Remember that the Israelites do not own the land, God does. Life in the land is inextricably tied to the mission God has given Israel. This mission is part of God's plan to draw the whole world to God, as the world sees the beauty of Israel's life with God. When the Israelites abandon that mission, when Israel's life with God becomes distorted and ugly and threatens to distort the world's view of God, they are exiled from the land.

The Promised Land provides the people of God with a home and a sense of place within which they can embody the mission God has given them: to live with God in such a compelling and fascinating way that the world is drawn to God. The Israelites are called to do the hard work of remembering (and continuing to remember) that their relationship with God is the source of their identity as a people and the reason for their presence in the land. The temptation of life in the land is that the people of God can become so comfortable with that life, it becomes disconnected from life with God and God's mission. Comfort becomes complacency; complacency breeds idolatry and injustice; idolatry and injustice (especially oppression of the poor) leads to exile.

Read: Leviticus 25:1-12

The Lord spoke to Moses on Mount Sinai, saying, "Speak to the Israelites and say to them: When you enter the land that I am giving you, the land shall observe a Sabbath for the Lord. Six years you shall sow your field, and six years you shall prune your vineyard and gather in their yield, but in the seventh year there shall be a Sabbath of complete rest for the land, a Sabbath for the Lord: you shall not sow your field or prune your vineyard. You shall not reap the aftergrowth of your harvest or gather the grapes of your unpruned vine: it shall be a year of complete rest for the land. You may eat what the land yields during its Sabbath—you, your male and female slaves, your hired and your bound laborers who live with you, for your livestock also, and for the wild animals in your land all its yield shall be for food.

You shall count off seven weeks of years, seven times seven years, so that the period of seven weeks of years gives forty-nine years. Then you shall have the trumpet sounded loud; on the tenth day of the seventh month—on the Day of Atonement—you shall have the trumpet sounded throughout all your land. And you shall hallow the fiftieth year, and you shall proclaim liberty throughout the land to all its inhabitants. It shall be a Jubilee for you: you shall return, every one of you, to your property and every one of you to your family. That fiftieth year shall be a Jubilee for you: you shall not sow or reap the aftergrowth or harvest the unpruned vines. For it is a Jubilee; it shall be holy to you: you shall eat only what the field itself produces.

Additional Reading: Leviticus 25:13-55

Questions to Ponder

1. Have you ever witnessed or experienced the kind of sharing and generosity typical of the Jubilee? What were the particular circumstances?

2. Are there times when you have been drawn to God by the ways in which a person or group has regarded their possessions? Explain.

3. When outsiders look at the church generally, do you think they see sharing, generosity, and hospitality as hallmarks of the Christian life? Why or why not?

4. Is your congregation a comfortable home for you? How might you know if complacency has replaced comfort?

Closing Prayer

Lord, we are rich in goods and possessions.

We pray that you would protect us from setting our hope on the uncertainty of riches. Help us to place our hope in you, who richly provides us with everything for our enjoyment. Shape us so that we may be rich in good deeds, generous and ready to share through the grace of your Holy Spirit.

Amen.

Adapted from 1 Timothy 6:17-18

Chapter Seven

Holiness

Opening Prayer

Dear Jesus, help me to spread your fragrance everywhere. Flood my soul with your spirit and life. Penetrate and possess my whole being so utterly that all my life is a radiance of yours. Shine through me and be in me so that every person I come in contact with may feel your Presence in my soul. Let them look up and see no longer me but only You.

Attributed to St. John Henry Newman

Setting the Scene

Even after they enter and occupy the Promised Land, Israel's life with God and with each other is a process of formation, a process which can be instructive for Christians, too. Unlike the previous chapters, the themes of this chapter are not confined to a single book or chapter of scripture. Instead, we will draw on a variety of texts from the Old Testament. One could easily substitute other texts for those we will examine here. These texts represent a significant and widespread set of themes and episodes in God's drama of redemption.

We begin with God's declaration, "You shall be holy because I am holy" (Leviticus 19:2). This seems like a rather tall order, and it is. If we have any strong reactions to holiness, they are often negative ones. Both inside and outside the church we are pretty quick to detect and reject self-acquired holiness as nothing more than superficial airs of piety.

(Nobody described this false type of holiness better than the writer Flannery O'Connor. You might enjoy reading her short story, "Revelation," as preparation for this chapter.) Given the abundance of pseudo-holiness in our world, can we think about and attempt to embody a more authentic sort of holiness? To do so we will need to think about holiness in the light of our previous chapters.

It is not uncommon for Christians to think of holiness as being "set apart." Holy things or holy people are set apart from more everyday forms, uses, or activities. The connection between holiness and being set apart is deeper than simply putting something to one side. For example, to be holy as God is holy requires times or periods when we are set apart. This recognizes that holiness does not come naturally to us; quite the opposite. Our everyday lives and routines on their own often do not provide the right sort of contexts for us to deepen our love of God and neighbor. Think of those times when Jesus goes off by himself to pray as a way of renewing his mission. He encourages his followers to do likewise at times (Mark 6:31). Holiness seems to require that we spend time in set apart contexts.

When the seraphim in Isaiah 6 proclaim that the LORD is "holy, holy, holy," (Isaiah 6:1-4), they reflect the fact that the LORD's holiness, by its very nature, sets God apart. These two examples indicate that being "set apart" is sometimes more like a *precondition* for developing holiness; sometimes it is the *result* of being holy.

Being set apart is integral to holiness but may not say quite enough for us. The claim "You shall be holy because I am holy," indicates that holiness is a quality of God which God wants for us. Holiness is not simply a demand; it is one of God's desires for us. We can see the importance of this if we remember that our participation in the drama of God's redemption of the world is both preparation for and sharing in an ever-deepening friendship with God. God's ultimate desire for us is the type of unbroken intimacy that characterized life in the Garden and that will characterize life in the New Jerusalem.

Holiness, then, is tied to God's desire for friendship with us. There are many types of friendships, but friendships of the best sort are based on holding important things in common—having a common love and a common goal. God's call to holiness is an invitation to love what God loves. In this way our growth in holiness enables us to enjoy a deeper level of friendship with the one who is "Holy, Holy, Holy," (Isaiah 6:3; Revelation 4:8). In a world that persistently refuses to love what God loves, pursuing this type of holiness will inevitably set one apart.

If we think about holiness as loving what God loves, we might find some concrete examples of this idea in the Sermon on the Mount (Matthew 5-7). In the first verses of Matthew 5, Jesus proclaims what we know as the "Beatitudes." These verses are distinguished by their repeated use of the term "blessed." (e.g. Blessed are the poor in spirit for theirs is the kingdom of heaven. . . . Blessed are the peacemakers for they shall be called children of God . . .) These are not direct commands to become poor in spirit or peacemakers. Rather, they are a concise list of some citizens of the kingdom of God who are highly valued and loved by God. If we are to become holy, we are invited to love these people, too. Indeed, loving the peacemakers, for example, may actually help form us to become peacemakers. That is, loving those whom God loves will often entail an invitation to become like them.

Even if we understand the important role holiness plays in fitting us for friendship with God, it does not remove the fact that holiness is not one of our natural tendencies. Remember that we humans, through our sin, have damaged (but not obliterated) our friendship with God and our capacities for holiness. Nevertheless, through Christ, God has restored our capacities for holiness. Holiness, then, is both God's call to us and one of God's gracious gifts in Christ.

Even so, we should not think of our holiness as a one-time achievement, as a state of being we reach once and abide in forever. Rather, holiness is more like a muscle. The more it is exercised the larger it gets, becoming stronger and more flexible. It is, however, easy to confuse conventional signs of piety such as church going, hymn singing, tithing and public praying with true holiness. Holiness is connected to these and many other practices, but it cannot be reduced to them. True holiness manifests itself in the comprehensive devotion of our attention, words, and deeds to God. As the prophets of Israel repeatedly stress, proper forms of worship, apart from daily attention to justice and compassion, do not please God (see Amos 5:21-24). This is not to diminish the importance of offerings and prayer and worship. Rather it is to recognize that holiness involves the whole of life. Happily, then, as we grow in holiness in one aspect of our lives, it tends to lead us to grow in other areas, too. Also, as Amos makes very clear, failure in one area tends to cause failure in other areas, too. As we will see in the next chapter, this is one of the things that makes idolatry so insidious.

Read: Deuteronomy 7:6-8

For you are a people holy to the Lord your God; the Lord your God has chosen you out of all the peoples on earth to be his people, his treasured possession.

"It was not because you were more numerous than any other people that the Lord set his heart on you and chose you, for you were the fewest of all peoples. It was because the Lord loved you and kept the oath that he swore to your ancestors that the Lord has brought you out with a mighty hand and redeemed you from the house of slavery, from the hand of Pharaoh king of Egypt.

Additional Reading: Isaiah 6:1-3; Amos 5:21-24

Questions to Ponder

1. How is holiness is described in our culture and in the church? Do these descriptions square with what the Bible means by holiness? Or do they differ?

2. What would it mean to desire holiness for yourself or your congregation? What would such holy living look like? Is it possible to live a holy life all by yourself?

3. Are there particular aspects of your congregation's life and worship that help you cultivate true holiness? Are there other aspects that might be a hindrance to true holiness? Give concrete examples and explain your reasons.

Closing Prayer

You are to be praised, O God, in Zion:
to you shall vows be performed in Jerusalem.
To you who hears prayer shall all flesh come,
because of their transgressions.
Our sins are stronger than we are,
but you will blot them out.
Happy are they whom you choose
and draw to your courts to dwell there!
They will be satisfied by the beauty of your house,
by the holiness of your temple.
Teach us to love you, LORD, and to love your holiness.

Amen.

Adapted from Psalm 65:1-4

Chapter Eight

Idolatry

Opening Prayer

Take, O Lord, and receive my entire liberty, my memory, my understanding and my whole will. All that I am and all that I possess, You have given me: I surrender it all to You to be disposed of according to Your will. Give me only Your love and Your grace; with these I will be rich enough and will desire nothing more.

St. Ignatius of Loyola

Setting the Scene

Although Israel is called to holiness, the people repeatedly turn to idolatry. Whether connected or not, idolatry is often accompanied by manifest failure to keep the other commandments. Idolatry is also associated with unjust social structures and oppression of the vulnerable. Despite warnings from various prophets, it becomes apparent that idolatry is a difficult habit to recognize and an even harder habit to break. Israel's idolatry brings God's judgment. This judgment often takes the form of military reversals or defeats at the hands of the surrounding peoples. Most disastrously, this happens when the northern kingdom is defeated by the Assyrians in 722 B.C.E. The southern kingdom of Judah is defeated by the Babylonians in 586 B.C.E. The remaining Judean aristocracy is taken into exile. The bulk of the peasant population, along with the old and the sick, is left behind to scratch out a living by whatever means they can. The Temple in Jerusalem is destroyed and it appears the covenant is in jeopardy.

In future chapters, you will examine how God's steadfast love for Israel shines through even Israel's idolatry and the judgment that such idolatry brings. Idolatry, however, is the focus of this chapter. It is probably safe to assume that none of us has ever sacrificed an animal or anything else to a god. If that is primarily what idolatry is about, then it will seem very hard for modern people to identify with Israel's idolatry, to see it as something into which we, too, might fall.

One of the most important things to recognize about idolatry is that idolatry is easy. Still, it is also important to remember that nobody wakes up one morning, looks out the window, and decides then and there to become an idolater. Idolatry happens gradually, through a series of small, seemingly benign or even prudent decisions we make over time. These decisions slowly and gradually divert our attention away from God.

Here is how we might imagine it happening: An Israelite farmer wishes to trade olives for wheat with his Moabite neighbor. They agree on terms, and then the Moabite informs the Israelite that Moabites always seal business deals with a sacrifice to one of their gods of commerce. The Israelite resists; the Moabite says he does not care if the Israelite believes in any of these gods, but insists that sacrifice is necessary to seal the deal. The Israelite relents. Nothing happens. No bolt of thunder from heaven strikes them dead. Over time, they continue to trade; both of them prosper. Perhaps they decide to merge their business interests by marrying the Israelite's son to the Moabite's daughter. Of course, weddings also require sacrifices. By this point, the Israelite is accustomed to compromising on these matters. After all, he doesn't really believe in Moabite gods. After the marriage, there is the question of how children will be raised. After watching his own father compromise his devotion to the one God of Israel, it is a straightforward matter for the son to do likewise. And so it goes. A series of clever business moves, a wise and prudent marriage, and a flexible parenting arrangement all work together to dilute and divert the attention of three generations of Israelites from the single-minded focus on God that their law commands.

Idolatry is not so much a single decision to stray from the worship of Israel's God to another god or gods. Rather, idolatry is first and foremost a failure of attentiveness. When our attention on God lapses, we no longer see clearly how our day to day lives can draw us away from God. Indeed, if the prophets are correct, even if we do not formally abandon the worship of God, our day to day lives can draw us so far away from God that God no longer recognizes our worship. In such cases, God treats the Israelites worship as if it were no different from idolatry (see for example, Amos 5:21-27).

Jesus tells his followers that the first and greatest commandment is to "Love the Lord your God with all of your heart, all your soul and all your mind" (Matthew 22:37 quoting Deuteronomy 6:5). The rest of the passage in Deuteronomy speaks about how important it is to remember this commandment daily. This is because so many aspects of our lives--our jobs, families, hobbies, even our church commitments—can slowly work to divert our attention from God. When this happens, the stage is set for us to fall step by step into idolatry.

Read: Isaiah 58:3-7

"Why do we fast, but you do not see?
Why humble ourselves, but you do not notice?"
Look, you serve your own interest on your fast day
and oppress all your workers.
You fast only to quarrel and to fight
and to strike with a wicked fist.
Such fasting as you do today
will not make your voice heard on high.
Is such the fast that I choose,
a day to humble oneself?
Is it to bow down the head like a bulrush
and to lie in sackcloth and ashes?
Will you call this a fast,
a day acceptable to the Lord?
Is not this the fast that I choose:
to loose the bonds of injustice,
to undo the straps of the yoke,
to let the oppressed go free,
and to break every yoke?
Is it not to share your bread with the hungry
and bring the homeless poor into your house;
when you see the naked, to cover them
and not to hide yourself from your own kin?

Additional Reading: Amos 5:21-24; Micah 6:8

Questions to Ponder

1. How do these passages characterize the differences between true holiness and the mere appearance of holiness?

2. Why do you think this distinction is important in our own lives of discipleship?

3. Can you think of an example from your life when a series of seemingly small and benign decisions led you to compromise something important about your faith? Explain.

4. What things or activities in your daily life most distract you from God?

5. What aspects of your congregation's life and worship are particularly helpful in keeping your attention regularly focused on God? How specifically do you find these helpful?

Closing Prayer

Lord, create in us a deep and persistent desire for you so that we may say with the Psalmist: "As the deer longs for the water-brooks, so longs my soul for you, O God. My soul is athirst for God, athirst for the living God; when shall I come to appear before the presence of God?"

adapted from Psalm 42:1-2

Chapter Nine

Steadfast Love

Opening Prayer

Make a joyful noise to the LORD, all the earth.
Worship the LORD with gladness; come into his presence with singing.
Know that the LORD is God.
It is he that made us, and we are his; we are his people, and the sheep of his pasture.
Enter his gates with thanksgiving, and his courts with praise.
Give thanks to him, bless his name.
For the LORD is good; his steadfast love endures forever, and his faithfulness to all generations.

Psalm 100:1-5

Setting the Scene

Because idolatry often happens gradually and in the midst of regular patterns of worship, it is difficult for the people of God to recognize their own idolatry once they slip into it. God sent prophets to point out the ways in which Israel's life and worship had deviated from what God desired.

One of the primary tasks for the prophet is to confront the people of God with the ways in which God views them and their actions, as opposed to the ways they view themselves. It is a bracing form of truth-telling. Building on this confrontation, prophets urge repentance, declare the consequences of failing to repent, and always reaffirm God's steadfast love.

For the most part, the people of God did not recognize or accept the prophets' message; their idolatry blinded them to the real state of their relationship with God. Therefore, they felt no need to change their ways. This is one of the great ironies reflected in prophetic literature: At those times when we are most in need of a word from a prophet, we are least able to recognize and respond well to what the prophet says.

Repeated rejection of prophetic warnings brings about God's judgment on the Israelites. The most decisive form of that judgment is military defeat and exile at the hands of Israel's enemies. These events are also foreseen by the prophets.

Christians may, and perhaps should, feel uneasy with notions of God's judgment. It is good to wrestle with this aspect of scripture. Here are two quick thoughts about God's judgment of Israel as detailed in the Old Testament. The first relates to God's judgment on a macro level. We should be very slow to presume we know what God can, will, and ought to do. When God acts contrary to our expectations, it is a call to us to reflect and not to make hasty assumptions. The second thought is on a more micro level. We should not think of ancient Israel as a nation living at ease among a host of peace-loving nations. Israel lies in a strategic location between conflicting world powers, be they Assyria, Egypt, Babylon, Persia, or Rome. Conflict and violence are considered normal. We might take Israel's sustained existence over time as the result of God's direct protection. When God's relentless love and constant invitation to love in return is persistently rejected or ignored, judgment follows. Instead of God actively leading an assault on Israel, Israel's demise might be more the result of God's withdrawal of protection in response to Israel's sin.

Even when the prophets are proclaiming God's judgment on the people of God, there are also promises of restoration and redemption. God's covenant with the people is everlasting. There is nothing that Israel can do to stop God's love for and commitment to them. These promises of redemption are particular reminders of God's steadfast love, a love that cannot be broken.

Indeed, the Psalmist reminds us that God's "steadfast love is better than life" (Psalm 63:3).

We have all probably had the experience of making promises or commitments we regret. Even when we have promised freely and willingly, we get to the point when it is our turn to live up to our end of the bargain, and we find that we would prefer to do almost anything else. Nevertheless, because of our well-developed sense of duty, or a concern over our personal integrity, or because we fear the consequences, we go ahead and fulfill our obligations. It is not so with God.

Much of the story of scripture can be told as the story of God's faithfulness to the promises God made to Abraham and his kin. We will misunderstand a central aspect of this story and a fundamental part of God's character, however, if we think of God's faithfulness in terms of our own commitments to our promises. God does not stick by Israel because God must. God is not boxed into a corner by God's own rash promises in the ways that we might find ourselves boxed into a corner. God is faithful to Israel because God loves Israel. Although it is true that the faithfulness that comes from obligation is better than unfaithfulness, the faithfulness that overflows from God's love is better than life itself.

This is particularly astonishing in the light of Israel's persistent turning away from God. Repeatedly throughout scripture, however, it becomes clear there is nothing the people of Israel can do to stop God from loving them. That love is what generated God's promises in the first place. Even when God's love is reflected in judgment of Israel, that judgment is designed to restore and renew Israel's relationship with God. It is God's steadfast love that promises the redemption and restoration of Israel, so that all the nations will be blessed because of what they see in this extraordinary love that God shows to Israel.

When presented with a scenario such as this, Christians typically have two related questions: First, doesn't God love everybody equally? Secondly, what does this love for Israel have to do with the church?

The first question can be answered fairly directly here. We can begin to answer the second question here, but it will also come up in some of our future chapters. Yes, God loves all humans. This is part of what it means in Genesis 1:26 when God creates humans in the image of God. Moreover, this is not a half-hearted love. God loves humans without hesitation or reserve and there is nothing humans can do to stop God loving them.

However, this truth can remain abstract. As it turns out, scripture reveals that God wills to love us in a very particular way. Remember that God does not need to create; God's creation flows out of God's love. That love creates us for *shalom* in the garden. That love also calls Abraham to be the father of a particular people and to be a blessing to the nations. In and through that love, God wills to become bound to Israel through an everlasting covenant. As we will soon see, God brings that covenant to its climax in the life, death, and resurrection of Jesus. That, too, is a specific way in which God's love for all is revealed to all (John 3:16). God's steadfast love of Israel, therefore, does not override God's love for all. Rather, it is one of the specific ways in which God's love for all humanity is revealed.

As noted above, the answer to the second question will require a bit more unpacking. At this point it will have to suffice to say that God's everlasting covenant with Israel is not broken or overridden but rather fulfilled in the church. This, then, binds the church to Israel (though not to the nation-state of the same name) in complex ways that we will explore in future chapters.

Even in the midst of judgment, God's steadfast love for the people of God includes a promise of future redemption. This promise invites, and perhaps encourages, hopes and expectations for when, how, and through whom the redemption of the people of God will take place. For many Jews at the time of Jesus's birth, this expectation of redemption was focused on a specific figure, the Messiah. There are allusions to this type of figure in the prophets (e.g. Daniel 7; Isaiah 42:3; Zechariah 9:9) and other non-canonical Jewish texts of the period (see the Dead Sea Scrolls [4Q 176; 4QFlor 458]). At the same time, Jewish expectations about the Messiah are quite diverse. In the gospels, we read of numerous ways Jesus does and does not fit with the messianic expectations of his fellow Jews. As much as the New

Testament writers present Jesus as the climactic fulfillment of God's engagement with Israel, they also consistently maintain it is only through an encounter with the living Jesus that one comes to believe he is the Messiah of Israel.

Read: Exodus 19:4-6

'You have seen what I did to the Egyptians and how I bore you on eagles' wings and brought you to myself. Now, therefore, if you obey my voice and keep my covenant, you shall be my treasured possession out of all the peoples. Indeed, the whole earth is mine, but you shall be for me a priestly kingdom and a holy nation.' These are the words that you shall speak to the Israelites."

Additional Reading: Psalm 103, 107, 136; Ezekiel 34:10-16; Hosea 11:1-4

Questions to Ponder

1. According to these passages, what are some different ways the people of God come to know and experience God's steadfast love?

2. God and Israel have a history. How is God's steadfast love revealed in that history?

3. What are some of the ways you experience God's steadfast love in day-to-day life? Try to be as specific as you can.

4. Are there also times when you have known God's love in and through dramatic or climactic events?

5. What are some dimensions of your congregation's life and worship that connect you to God's steadfast love? Again, seek to be specific.

Closing Prayer

O Lord, because your steadfast love is better than life, our lips will praise you. We will bless you as long as we live; we will lift up our hands and call on your name. Our souls are satisfied as with a rich feast, and our mouths praise you with joyful lips when we think of you in our beds and meditate on you in the watches of the night. Our soul clings to you; your right hand upholds us. We thank you for your steadfast love.

Amen.

Adapted from Psalm 63:3-8

Chapter Ten

Jesus, the Redeemer of Israel

Opening Prayer

O come, O come, Emmanuel
and ransom captive Israel
that mourns in lonely exile here
until the Son of God appear.

O come, Thou Wisdom from on high,
Who orderest all things far and nigh;
To us the path of knowledge show
And teach us in her ways to go.

O come, Thou Rod of Jesse, free
Thine down from Satan's tyranny;
From depths of hell Thy people save
And give them victory over the grave.

O come, Thou Key of David, come,
And open wide our heavenly home;
Make safe the way that leads on high
And close the path to misery.

> John Mason Neale (translator)

Setting the Scene

For Christians, the life, death, and resurrection of Jesus mark the climax—but not the endpoint—of God's action in bringing the world to its proper end. It is, therefore, also the climax, but not the end, of God's dealings with the people of Israel. In this chapter and those that follow, we will not explore the gospel accounts from beginning to end. Rather, we will explore the contours of a framework within which we Christians can read the gospels in ways that enhance our understanding of and participation in God's drama of salvation.

Paul tells us, "when the fullness of time had come, God sent his son," (Galatians 4:4). We do not know all that accounted for the "fullness of time." We do know that that world into which Jesus was born was controlled by Rome. The land promised by God to the people of Israel was, yet again, under the control of a world power. There were diverse and complex hopes around when, how, and by what means God would bring about the redemption of Israel. Into this world and into these hopes Jesus is born.

For the most part, the Romans liked to rule through trusted local authorities. Herod the Great (37-4 B.C.E) was one such ruler. Herod was in charge when Jesus was born and died shortly after Jesus's birth. He was succeeded by his son, Archelaus. Archelaus proved to be an inept and vicious ruler. Hence, by the time of Jesus's death, the Romans had installed one of their own, Pontius Pilate, as governor.

Although we do not know exactly what "fulfills the time" from God's perspective, we do know that Roman occupation presented the Jews of Jesus's day with a rather acute question: How should the people of God live faithfully before God while also under Roman occupation? As one might imagine, Jews developed a variety of answers to this question, ranging from accommodation to violent resistance, and most things in-between. Hovering in the background of most of Jesus's engagements with his fellow Jews in the gospels is this question about faithful life before God.

The beginnings of stories often tell us crucial things about their chief characters. The gospels are no different with regard to their chief character, Jesus. Among the four gospels in the New Testament, Matthew and Luke contain accounts of Jesus's birth. These gospels show very little interest in the actual birth process. Rather, they devote a great deal of space to fitting the birth of Jesus into the ongoing drama of God's dealings with Israel within the Roman context. In speaking of Jesus's beginnings as they do, the gospels point us in the directions we should look in order to understand and respond to the subsequent life, death, and resurrection of Jesus.

The accounts of Jesus's birth remind us that Jesus comes as the redeemer of Israel and not, in the first instance, to start a separate religion called *Christianity*. Christians are reminded of this each time they call Jesus "the Christ." *Christ* is the English form of the Greek word *Christos*. *Christos* is the Greek translation of the Hebrew *meshiach*, or Messiah. To call Jesus the Christ is to identify him as the Messiah, the redeemer of Israel. Once we recognize this connection, readers of the gospels are invited to have our understanding of what it means to be Israel's redeemer shaped by the subsequent words and deeds and death and resurrection of Jesus. At the same time, we are challenged to grant Jesus's words and deeds authority, because we already know who he is. In answer to the question of how to live faithfully before God in the particular context Jesus shares with all his Jewish contemporaries, Jesus's answers will trump all others, because he is "Emmanuel, God with us," (Matthew 1:23).

Read: Luke 1:46-55

And Mary said,
"My soul magnifies the Lord,
and my spirit rejoices in God my Savior,
for he has looked with favor on the lowly state of his servant.

Surely from now on all generations will call me blessed,
for the Mighty One has done great things for me,
and holy is his name;
indeed, his mercy is for those who fear him
from generation to generation.
He has shown strength with his arm;
he has scattered the proud in the imagination of their hearts.
He has brought down the powerful from their thrones
and lifted up the lowly;
he has filled the hungry with good things
and sent the rich away empty.
He has come to the aid of his child Israel,
in remembrance of his mercy,
according to the promise he made to our ancestors,
to Abraham and to his descendants forever."

Additional Reading:
Luke 2:25-32; Matthew 3:13-17

Questions to Ponder

1. What do you think those who first heard these announcements might have expected from Jesus once full grown? How does reading these texts today shape your own thinking about the coming of Jesus into the world at Christmas?

2. Think of how our society celebrates the birth of Jesus. Do you think the way a society celebrates Christmas sets expectations about who we expect Jesus to be today? How might this be so?

3. How do these texts counter the cultural norms and practices associated with Christ's birth?

4. How does your church prepare for and celebrate the birth of Jesus? In what ways are the themes in these texts from Luke and Matthew central to your celebration of Christmas?

5. How does your church's preparation and celebration help you to understand Jesus better? How does it shape your discipleship?

Closing Prayer

Almighty God, you have poured upon us
the new light of your incarnate Word:
Grant that this light, enkindled in our hearts,
may shine forth in our lives;
through Jesus Christ our Lord,
who lives and reigns with you

in the unity of the Holy Spirit,
one God, now and forever.

Amen.

Collect for the 1st Sunday of Christmas
Book of Common Prayer

Chapter Eleven
Death and Resurrection

Opening Prayer

Lord Jesus Christ, you stretched out your arms of love on the hard wood of the cross that everyone might come within your saving embrace: So clothe us in your Spirit that we, reaching forth our hands in love, may bring those who do not know you to the knowledge and love of you; for the honor of your Name.

Amen.

Collect for Morning Prayer
Book of Common Prayer

Setting the Scene

Remember that we began this book by looking at the beginning of salvation's history (creation) and the end (restoration) in quick succession. We will follow the same pattern with regard to Jesus. Of course, the life and teaching of Jesus are crucial for Christians. Reading and studying the gospels should be a regular part of a Christian's life. Nevertheless, this book has focused on a framework for scripture and ways such a framework can shape and enliven our reading of it.

Having briefly covered the birth and beginnings of Jesus in the previous chapter, here we focus on his death and resurrection. Christians have a variety of ways for faithfully understanding the significance of the death and resurrection of Jesus; we will examine some of the most common and important ways without assuming we have looked at everything that can be said. Indeed, as John's gospel reminds us, "If everything Jesus did were written down, I suppose the world itself could not contain the books that would be written," (21:20).

Although the first century was very different from our own, we can be confident that the Roman authorities would not crucify you for wandering around the countryside urging everyone to love their neighbors. Nevertheless, the Romans did crucify Jesus. Moreover, they did so with the approval of both the Jewish leaders in Jerusalem and at least a portion of the population of Jerusalem.

These three groups were probably opposed to Jesus for different but overlapping reasons. The Romans were concerned about anybody who might threaten the civil order. Anyone who drew crowds in the way that Jesus did was suspicious. They probably did not care very much about what he was teaching. The fact that he was gathering large crowds of Jews in Jerusalem at a particularly volatile time would have been enough to get the attention of the Roman authorities.

The Jewish authorities were concerned because they understood the radical implications of the words and deeds of Jesus. For example, when Jesus chases those selling sacrificial animals and those changing money from the Temple, he was not primarily making a statement about the presence of commercial interests in a religious place. Rather, he was symbolically (and temporarily) shutting down the sacrificial system. He was in effect claiming that one need no longer offer sacrifices for one's sins because the Messiah was at hand, freely offering God's forgiveness. The Temple was no longer needed as a place of sacrifice because the Son of God was at hand. Recall also Jesus's forgiveness of the paralytic at the beginning of his ministry (Matt 9:2-8; Mark 2:1-12; Luke 5:17-26). There again, Jesus acts as if he can freely administer God's forgiveness apart from the recognized practices of repentance and sacrifice in the Temple.

Forgiveness of sins outside of the system of sacrifice in the Temple is one, but by no means the only, way in which Jesus's actions and words made it clear to his Jewish contemporaries that he was claiming to be the Messiah, Emmanuel, God with us, and that people should respond appropriately and follow him. From the perspective of other devout Jews such as the Pharisees, Jesus was a dangerous heretic, teaching falsehoods regarding the most important matters of Jewish faith and practice.

The views of the groups of people who turn against Jesus are harder to discern. Crowds were seen as notoriously fickle in the ancient world and easily manipulated. No doubt for some Jesus simply failed to live up to their expectations of what the Messiah should be and do. They were disappointed with Jesus's failure to live up to their expectations. Recall the words of the two disciples on the road to Emmaus when they are speaking with their strange companion who turns out to be the resurrected Christ, "We were hoping that he was the one to redeem Israel" (Luke 24:21).

When Jesus dies on the cross, the Romans are rid of a troublemaker and the Jewish leaders are confirmed in their judgment that this man was a heretic and deceiver of the people. Of course, the resurrection changes all that. First and foremost, the resurrection is God's vindication of the life, teachings, and freely willed self-offering of Jesus. The resurrection is the decisive instance of the Father shouting to the world, "This is my beloved Son in whom I am well pleased."

In addition to these ways of looking at the resurrection, the New Testament writers take the resurrection to be the climactic moment in God's restoration of shalom as all things become reconciled to God in Christ (2 Corinthians 5:16-21). The resurrection testifies to the ultimate defeat of death and its power over us (Romans 5:12-21; 1 Corinthians 15:50-56). The resurrection confirms that Jesus is Lord and that all things will ultimately be subjected to him (Philippians 2:9-11; 1 Corinthians 15:20-28). The resurrection bears witness to the fact that in Christ God's promise to Abraham to bless all the nations is fulfilled as Jews and Gentiles are joined into one new body in Christ (Ephesians 2:11-22). The vindication of Jesus who freely takes on suffering in obedience to God is a sign that God will also vindicate the suffering that believers willingly take on in obedience to Christ (1 Peter 2:20-25). Finally, Jesus's offering of his life back to God in obedience to the Father's will is taken to be a sacrificial offering that ends all future sacrificial offerings (Hebrews 9:26-28; 10:10-12).

Read: Hebrews 1:1-4

Long ago God spoke to our ancestors in many and various ways by the prophets, but in these last days he has spoken to us by a Son, whom he appointed heir of all things, through whom he also created the worlds. He is the reflection of God's glory and the exact imprint of God's very being, and he sustains all things by his powerful word.

When he had made purification for sins, he sat down at the right hand of the Majesty on high, having become as much superior to angels as the name he has inherited is more excellent than theirs.

Additional Reading: Romans 1:1-6

Questions to Ponder

1. How do these texts connect Jesus's resurrection to God's being as triune? What about the connection between the resurrection and history of Israel?

2. Where do you see in these passages from Hebrews and Romans something of the overarching framework we've been suggesting in this study?

3. Does your congregation emphasize (or de-emphasize) particular aspects of the resurrection? If so, which ones? How is this emphasis played out in your life together?

4. Do you personally tend to emphasize (or de-emphasize) particular aspects of the resurrection? How do they impact your understanding of Jesus and how you live out your faith?

5. How does your congregation celebrate the resurrection? (You do not have to limit yourself to Easter here).

6. How do those celebrations help you understand Christ's resurrection?

Closing Prayer

Alleluia, alleluia.
Christ, rising again from the dead, dies now no more:
death shall no more have dominion over him; for in that he died, he died once:
but in that he lives, he lives unto God, alleluia, alleluia.

Amen.

Adapted from Romans 6:9-10

Chapter Twelve

The Spirit and Scripture

Opening Prayer

O God, the Holy Ghost,
who art light unto thine elect: Evermore enlighten us.
Thou who art fire of love, Evermore enkindle us.
Thou who art Lord and Giver of Life, Evermore live in us.
Thou who bestowest sevenfold grace,
Evermore replenish us.
As the wind is thy symbol,
So forward our goings.
As the dove, so launch us heavenwards.
As water, so purify our spirits.
As a cloud, so abate our temptations.
As dew, so revive our languor.
As fire, so purge our dross.

Christina Rossetti

Setting the Scene

This will be the final chapter in this book, and so it is fitting to conclude with the Holy Spirit. As we saw with the resurrection, there are numerous and profound ways to think about the Spirit. For our purposes, we will focus on two aspects of the Spirit's work.

The resurrection is the climactic moment in God's drama of salvation. It provides the conclusive testimony that God's plan to restore the *shalom* of creation involved taking on human flesh, living and dying as one of us, and conquering death in the resurrection. Although this marks the climax of God's drama, the last act—the full restoration of *shalom* in the New Jerusalem (which we examined in chapters 3 and 4)—has yet to be enacted. Christians today live in a world marked by the resurrection on the one hand, and, on the other, by the movement in God's time toward the consummation of all things, when "the kingdoms of this world will become the kingdom of our God and of his Christ," (Revelation 11:15). In this time between resurrection and consummation, Christians are called to live out their lives in Christ as the church. The pouring out of the Spirit upon the believers at the feast of Pentecost is traditionally seen as the birthday of the church (Acts 2:1-47).

The presence of the Spirit in the lives and communities of these first believers confirmed for them that the resurrected Christ had not abandoned them. They belonged to Christ and Christ promised not to leave them without his presence in the form of the Holy Spirit. Thus, the first thing to note about the Spirit is that the Spirit is God's gift to the Church to aid, encourage, guide, direct and empower believers as they negotiate their way through the world. This leads to the second aspect of the Spirit's presence that will be particularly relevant to this chapter.

The confessional documents of all the large Christian denominations recognize the importance the role the Spirit plays in reading, interpreting, and embodying scripture. Indeed, it would appear that all Christians grant that the Spirit plays a significant role in all true scriptural interpretation. This is so, even if these documents do not really spell out *how* the Spirit plays this role or how to discern Spirit directed interpretation from other sorts. We will not resolve these large matters here. We can, however, begin to think about the role of the Spirit in reading scripture by briefly examining some themes in John's gospel.

In his last meal with his disciples, Jesus promises them that the Spirit will help them to carry on as faithful followers after his death, resurrection, and ascension (John 14:18). Jesus promises that the Spirit will enable the disciples to "remember all that I have said to you," (14:26). Moreover, Jesus indicates he has more to say that the disciples simply cannot bear yet. The Spirit will make these things known, too (16:12–15). Reminding and speaking of what is "more" are activities of the Spirit that enable the followers of Jesus to continue the mission Jesus started, and we are to continue.

Remembering the words of Jesus, however, is not simply a feat of Spirit-inspired memory. For example, in John 2:13-25, Jesus goes to Jerusalem for Passover. He drives out the money changers and those selling sacrificial animals. This leads the disciples to "remember" Psalm 69:10, ("Zeal for your house will consume me,"). Later, when asked by what authority Jesus has done these things, he responds, "Destroy this temple, and in three days I will raise it up," (2:19). Although nobody seems to understand this comment at the time, John notes, "When, therefore, he was raised from the dead, his disciples *remembered* that he had said this; and they believed the scripture and the word which Jesus had spoken" (2:22, emphasis added).

We find an additional interesting example in John 12. As Jesus enters Jerusalem for the final time, there is great cheering. Jesus is welcomed as the "king of Israel" (12:13). Jesus rides into Jerusalem on a donkey, which leads John to reference a passage drawn from Zechariah 9:9: "Rejoice greatly, O daughter Zion! Shout aloud, O daughter Jerusalem! See, your king comes to you; triumphant and victorious is he, humble and riding on a donkey, on a colt, the foal of a donkey." We then read in John, "His disciples did not understand these things at first; but when Jesus was glorified, then they remembered these things that had been written of him and had been done to him," (12:16).

What seems to be the case is that although they did not understand Jesus's actions at the time, after the resurrection and the sending of the Spirit, the disciples come to understand Jesus's actions by means of the Old Testament citation *and* to understand the citation in the light of Jesus's actions. *Remembering* here involves being enabled by the Spirit to connect an event (Jesus's entry to Jerusalem) with a scriptural text (Zechariah 9:9) in ways that allow both events and text to be understood in new and unanticipated ways.

In each of these cases, the disciples only *remember* in the light of the resurrection. The act of remembrance the Spirit enables here is not so much an exercise in recollection as much as an understanding of things said and done in the past, from the perspective of the death and resurrection of Jesus.

Read: Acts 2:14-36

But Peter, standing with the eleven, raised his voice and addressed them, "Fellow Jews and all who live in Jerusalem, let this be known to you, and listen to what I say. Indeed, these are not drunk, as you suppose, for it is only nine o'clock in the morning. No, this is what was spoken through the prophet Joel:

'In the last days it will be, God declares,
that I will pour out my Spirit upon all flesh,
and your sons and your daughters shall prophesy,

and your young men shall see visions,
and your old men shall dream dreams.
Even upon my slaves, both men and women,
in those days I will pour out my Spirit,
and they shall prophesy.
And I will show portents in the heaven above
and signs on the earth below,
blood, and fire, and smoky mist.
The sun shall be turned to darkness
and the moon to blood,
before the coming of the Lord's great and glorious day.
Then everyone who calls on the name of the Lord shall be saved.'

"Fellow Israelites, listen to what I have to say: Jesus of Nazareth, a man attested to you by God with deeds of power, wonders, and signs that God did through him among you, as you yourselves know—this man, handed over to you according to the definite plan and foreknowledge of God, you crucified and killed by the hands of those outside the law. But God raised him up, having released him from the agony of death, because it was impossible for him to be held in its power. For David says concerning him,

'I saw the Lord always before me,
for he is at my right hand so that I will not be shaken;
therefore my heart was glad, and my tongue rejoiced;
moreover, my flesh will live in hope.

*For you will not abandon my soul to Hades
or let your Holy One experience corruption.
You have made known to me the ways of life;
you will make me full of gladness with your presence.'*

"Fellow Israelites, I may say to you confidently of our ancestor David that he both died and was buried, and his tomb is with us to this day. Since he was a prophet, he knew that God had sworn with an oath to him that he would put one of his descendants on his throne. Foreseeing this, David spoke of the resurrection of the Messiah, saying,

*'He was not abandoned to Hades,
nor did his flesh experience corruption.'*

"This Jesus God raised up, and of that all of us are witnesses. Being therefore exalted at the right hand of God and having received from the Father the promise of the Holy Spirit, he has poured out this that you see and hear. For David did not ascend into the heavens, but he himself says,

*'The Lord said to my Lord,
"Sit at my right hand,
until I make your enemies your footstool."'*

"Therefore let the entire house of Israel know with certainty that God has made him both Lord and Messiah, this Jesus whom you crucified."

Questions to Ponder

1. How does Peter link the old with the new in this sermon? Give specific examples.

2. What are the implications of this linking of old and new for your own practices of reading scripture and living faithfully?

3. What do you think is the Spirit's work in bringing together the old and the new?

4. What specific aspects of your congregation's life and worship help or encourage you to participate in the work of the Spirit? Explain.

Closing Prayer

Come, Holy Spirit, and send down from heaven the ray of your light. Come, Father of the poor, come, giver of gifts, come, light of our hearts. Best consoler, sweet host of the soul, sweet refresher; rest in work, shade in heat, comfort in tears. O blessed light, fill the innermost hearts of your faithful. Without you nothing is in us, nothing innocent. Wash what is soiled, water what is arid, heal what is wounded. Bend what is rigid, warm what is frigid, straighten what is crooked. Grant to your faithful who trust in you, your sevenfold holy gift: the reward of virtue, final salvation, eternal joy.

Amen, alleluia.

"Veni Sancte Spiritus," or "Come, Holy Spirit"

Conclusion

In the course of working through this material you have had a chance to piece together a framework within which you individually and as a congregation can, with the Spirit's help, read scripture as a whole--as something larger than the collection of books between two covers.

The goal of these studies is not primarily to dramatically alter the way you read scripture but rather to enhance and enrich what you already do. The large-scale overview offered here is not designed to stop close prayerful reading of individual verses. Instead, the hope is to help you fit discrete insights and observations into a larger whole. This larger whole aims to help you negotiate your way faithfully through the complex and changing contexts in which you live out your faith.

No doubt as you engage in ongoing study of scripture you will want to modify this framework, adjusting its contours and exchanging some of its emphases for others. These modifications will be a sign that the work you started here has been successful and that, like the scribe trained for the kingdom of God mentioned in Matthew 13:52, you can bring out of your treasure things old and new.

About the Author

Stephen Fowl is President and Dean of the Church Divinity School of the Pacific, engaged in the formation of the next generation of priests for the Episcopal Church. He is an internationally recognized scholar of the New Testament, focusing on the relationships between Scripture and Christian doctrine.

Thank you for reading
The Form of the Word:
Making Sense of Scripture in the Body of Christ!

If you enjoyed this book, please leave a review at Amazon or your favorite online retailer.

Connect with *The Englewood Review of Books*:

Website: englewoodreview.org

Facebook: facebook.com/erbks

Instagram: instagram.com/erbooks

Bluesky: https://bsky.app/profile/erbks.bsky.social

Other Books in the
Cultivating Communities Series:

The Shape of Our Lives: A Field Guide for Congregational Formation
by Philip D. Kenneson, Debra Dean Murphy, Jenny C. Williams,
Stephen E. Fowl, and James W. Lewis

The Virtue of Dialogue: Becoming a Thriving Church through Conversation
by C. Christopher Smith

Scan to the code to learn more about these books and other titles from Englewood Press!

Missio Alliance

www.ingramcontent.com/pod-product-compliance
Lightning Source LLC
Chambersburg PA
CBHW060530080526
44586CB00012B/684